WOMEN OF VALOR

GREAT WOMEN IN HISTORY

PragerU is redefining how people think about media and education. Watched millions of times every day, PragerU is the world's leading nonprofit with educational, entertaining, pro-American videos for every age. From intellectual, fact-based 5-Minute Videos and powerful personal storytelling to animated shows made just for kids—PragerU helps people of all ages think and live better.

PragerU Kids teaches history, civics, financial literacy, and American values to children across the K-12th grade spectrum. With kids shows, books, and educational resources for every grade, PragerU Kids offers content that parents and teachers trust and children love. Watch for free and learn more at PragerUkids.com.

Published by PragerU

15021 Ventura Boulevard #552

Sherman Oaks, CA 91403

WOMEN OF VALOR

Table of Contents

WOMEN OF VALOR

I was the 2nd
First Lady of the
United States!

ABIGAIL ADAMS

Meet Abigail Adams

Abigail Adams lived and helped shape an exciting time in world history: the founding of the United States of America.

In 1764, while the American colonies were still under British rule, Abigail married John Adams, a politically active Harvard-educated lawyer. He would go on to be a leader of the American Revolution and served as the first vice president under George Washington, our first president. When John became the second president, Abigail became the second First Lady of the United States!

Abigail had strong opinions about education, women's rights, and the abolition of slavery. She served as an unofficial advisor to her husband throughout their marriage. John was often away on business, so Abigail took charge at home. She managed the family's farm and finances while raising their children.

Interesting Fact

⭐ Born November 11 or 22, 1744 in Weymouth, Massachusetts (the calendar changed after she was born!).

⭐ Wife of John Adams (2nd U.S. president) and mother of John Quincy Adams (6th U.S. president).

⭐ First Lady of the United States (1797-1801).

⭐ **Advocate** for women's rights, education for all, and the **abolition** of slavery.

⭐ Died October 28, 1818 in Quincy, Massachusetts.

Young Abigail

Abigail was the second of four children, born to Reverend William Smith and Elizabeth Quincy Smith. She was raised on her family's farm in Massachusetts. Abigail often accompanied her mother to visit sick families in their community, bringing them food, clothing, and firewood.

During colonial times, girls could rarely attend school. So, Abigail's mother taught her math, reading, sewing, and cooking at home.

Abigail was very curious and loved reading the books in her father's large library. Her favorite subjects were philosophy, theology, ancient history, government, and law. As she grew older, Abigail and her friends discussed books they had read and exchanged letters about what they had learned.

Abigail's family hosted many well-educated guests, including her grandfather, Colonel John Quincy, who taught her about the importance of freedom and the value of public service. Abigail listened carefully and asked many questions to learn as much as she could about the world.

A New Life

When Abigail was 17, she met John Adams, a lawyer from the neighboring community of Braintree. During their two-year courtship, they wrote letters to each other to keep in touch. She began every letter with "Dearest Friend." John appreciated Abigail's intellect and perspective.

John and Abigail married in October 1764. They had six children, two of whom died young, which was very common in those days.

The family moved to Boston to be closer to John's work. There, they became friendly with many patriots including Samuel Adams and John Hancock.

John quickly became a leader in what would later become the American Revolution, and he was selected to attend the First Continental Congress in Philadelphia, Pennsylvania, in 1774.

Life in Boston in the 1770s

As tensions mounted between the American colonies and Great Britain, Boston became the center of growing unrest. During the Boston Massacre (1770), protesters insulted and threatened British soldiers in the streets of the city. The soldiers fired their muskets, killing several colonists.

During the Boston Tea Party (1773), American colonists dumped 342 chests of tea imported by the British East India Company into Boston Harbor. They were angry that the British Parliament had imposed a tax on tea, despite the fact that the American colonists had no **representation** in it. This was an example of one of the rallying cries of the American Revolution, "no taxation without representation."

The Revolutionary War

On April 19, 1775, British soldiers who were trying to destroy the colonists' military supplies were confronted by the Massachusetts militia. The fight was later known as the Battle of Lexington and Concord. While the colonists and the British tried to avoid a full-scale war, the battle turned out to be the opening shot of the American Revolutionary War.

Two months later, while John was away at the Second Continental Congress in Philadelphia, Abigail awoke to shaking and loud booms—the sound of cannon fire. She and her young son, John Quincy, climbed the hill behind their house to get a better view. They saw Boston Harbor full of smoke and flames as British warships **besieged** the city of Boston in what came to be known as the Battle of Bunker Hill. Abigail wrote about what she saw and sent the letters to her husband, who shared them with George Washington.

She wrote, "The constant roar of the cannon is so distressing that we cannot eat, drink, or sleep."

During the war, Abigail helped by hiding soldiers in her house and allowing them to train on her property. Money and goods were scarce, so she made her own soap and ink, spun cloth, and even melted pewter spoons to make **musket balls** for the soldiers.

Abigail managed the household and family finances while John was away, at a time when financial matters were considered a male responsibility.

Throughout their marriage, she and John continued to write letters to stay in touch. The letters comforted Abigail during John's long absences. Years later, they would help us understand what life was like in early America.

"Learning is not attained by chance, it must be sought for with ardor and attended to with diligence."

From Abigail Adams to her son John Quincy Adams (May 8, 1780)

Living Overseas

When the war ended in 1783, John moved to England to serve as the United States' Ambassador to Great Britain. John missed Abigail's political advice and support.

Finally, in 1784, Abigail and her daughter Nabby set sail for the month-long journey to Europe to join John and their son, John Quincy. There, Abigail met Thomas Jefferson. Although Abigail enjoyed her time in England and France, she longed to be home. The family returned to America in 1788, and John was elected the first vice president under George Washington.

Being First Lady

In 1796, when John Adams was elected president, Abigail became First Lady. She continued to advise her husband and played an active role in the discussion around America's early political parties. She defended John and his policies in letters to family and friends. In 1800, Abigail oversaw the family's move from Philadelphia to the new presidential mansion in Washington, D.C., which would later be known as the White House. They lived there for only four months.

DID YOU KNOW?

Abigail Adams wrote over 1,200 letters during her life, often sharing her opinions of life and politics, including her belief that women should have a voice in the government.

When John was meeting with his colleagues to draft the Declaration of Independence, Abigail asked him to:

"Remember the ladies and be more generous and favorable to them than your ancestors.

Throughout her life, Abigail supported education for girls

Retirement & Later Life

After John left office in 1801, he and Abigail returned to their home in Quincy, Massachusetts. Abigail spent time with family, supported her son's political career, and continued writing letters to many people, including Thomas Jefferson.

She died in 1818 of **typhoid fever** and did not live to see her son, John Quincy Adams, become president.

Fascinating Facts about Abigail

- Abigail was very devoted to her family. She missed her husband's presidential **inauguration** of 1797 in order to care for his sick mother!

- During a smallpox epidemic that threatened the early colonists, Abigail and her children tried a risky new treatment to prevent the disease: scraping a smallpox-infected serum into the skin. They survived, but many others did not.

- Abigail was one of the few First Ladies to be politically active prior to the 20th century. Some people called her "Mrs. President" because she had so much influence over John.

- Abigail spoke up for the fair treatment of government leaders by the press when she and her husband were attacked in the newspapers.

- After she became First Lady, Abigail defended the right of a black American boy named James to go to school. He was mistreated for having black skin, but Abigail declared that this violated "the Christian principle of doing to others as we should have others to us," and the head of the school apologized.

- Abigail and Barbara Bush are the only women to have both a husband and a son serve as an American president.

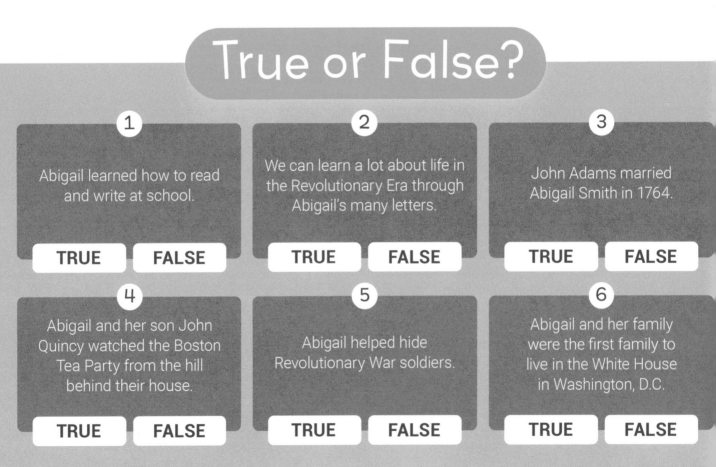

True or False?

1
Abigail learned how to read and write at school.

TRUE   FALSE

2
We can learn a lot about life in the Revolutionary Era through Abigail's many letters.

TRUE   FALSE

3
John Adams married Abigail Smith in 1764.

TRUE   FALSE

4
Abigail and her son John Quincy watched the Boston Tea Party from the hill behind their house.

TRUE   FALSE

5
Abigail helped hide Revolutionary War soldiers.

TRUE   FALSE

6
Abigail and her family were the first family to live in the White House in Washington, D.C.

TRUE   FALSE

Answer key in two pages

Word Search

ABIGAIL ADAMS
LETTERS
FIRST LADY
COLONISTS
EDUCATION
BOSTON
REVOLUTIONARY WAR
SOLDIERS
SMALLPOX
READING
ADVISOR
BUNKER HILL

Answer key on next page

```
C A C S M A L L P O X M O J M V P
B J U R N I R R F C E E F B J E A
S O A A M I B R E A D I N G J O G
U E S A N C O N B I U R A O O I Y
X E M T E U M V N A C G I D B S W
W M I H O V U I I P A K N E V O B
I Q O Q S N O P C X T T A Q K P U
S F I R S T L A D Y I A M U A B N
O E U A D V I S O R O A H G O P K
L M M F R P C O L O N I S T S S E
D R E V O L U T I O N A R Y W A R
I M T B Z L E T T E R S J H P E H
E T N L B Y M W X F R Y G S D M I
R A B I G A I L A D A M S N T V L
S G P U I O O C M O W U A D S T L
```

"Dearest Friend" Creative Writing Exercises

1. Write a letter to a friend or family member that you haven't seen in a long time.

Describe a recent event in your school or neighborhood. Write about something you learned or someone who inspired you. Share your opinions! Ask an adult for help to address and mail your letter.

2. Imagine that you could contact Abigail Adams.

Write her a letter and share something you learned about her life. What do you think might surprise Abigail about life in America in the 21st century? What question would you most like to ask her?

Glossary

- **Advocate:** One who argues for a cause; a supporter or defender.

- **Abolition:** The act of doing away with or the state of being done away with, as in the ending of slavery.

- **Representation:** The right of having a spokesperson for your interests in a governing body.

- **Besieged:** To surround and attack.

- **Musket Balls:** One of the earliest forms of bullets that were fired from muskets and rifles.

- **Typhoid Fever:** A highly infectious disease that's characterized by high fever, headache, coughing, and reddish spots on the skin.

- **Inauguration:** A formal ceremony that marks the beginning of service in public office.

Sources

Caroli, Betty Boyd. "Abigail Adams." *Encyclopedia Britannica*, 18 Nov. 2020, https://www.britannica.com/biography/Abigail-Adams. March 2021.

Ducksters. "Biography: Abigail Adams for Kids." *Ducksters, Technological Solutions, Inc. (TSI)*, www.ducksters.com/biography/women_leaders/abigail_adams.php. March 2021.

Holton, Woody. *Abigail Adams: A Life*. New York: Atria Books, 2010.

Massachusetts Historical Society, "Adams Family Papers: An Electronic Archive." *Massachusetts Historical Society*, www.masshist.org/digitaladams. March 2021.

National Park Service. "Abigail Adams Biography." *National Park Service*, 31 Mar. 2012, www.nps.gov/adam/abigailbio.htm.

Shafer, Ronald. "'A Fearsome Decision': Abigail Adams Had Her Children Inoculated against Smallpox." *MSN News*, 12 Dec. 2020, www.msn.com/en-us/news/us/a-fearsome-decision-abigail-adams-had-her-children-inoculated-against-smallpox/ar-BB1bRWbk.

The American Heritage Dictionary of the English Language (online edition). Boston: Houghton Mifflin Harcourt.

The National First Ladies' Library. "First Lady Biography: Abigail Adams." *The National First Ladies' Library*, http://www.firstladies.org/biographies/firstladies.aspx?biography=2. March 2021.

True, Kelley. *Who Was Abigail Adams?* New York: Grosset & Dunlap, 2014.

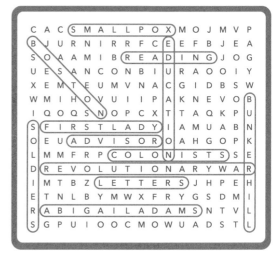

TRUE & FALSE KEY: 1. False. 2. True. 3. True. 4. False. 5. True. 6. True.

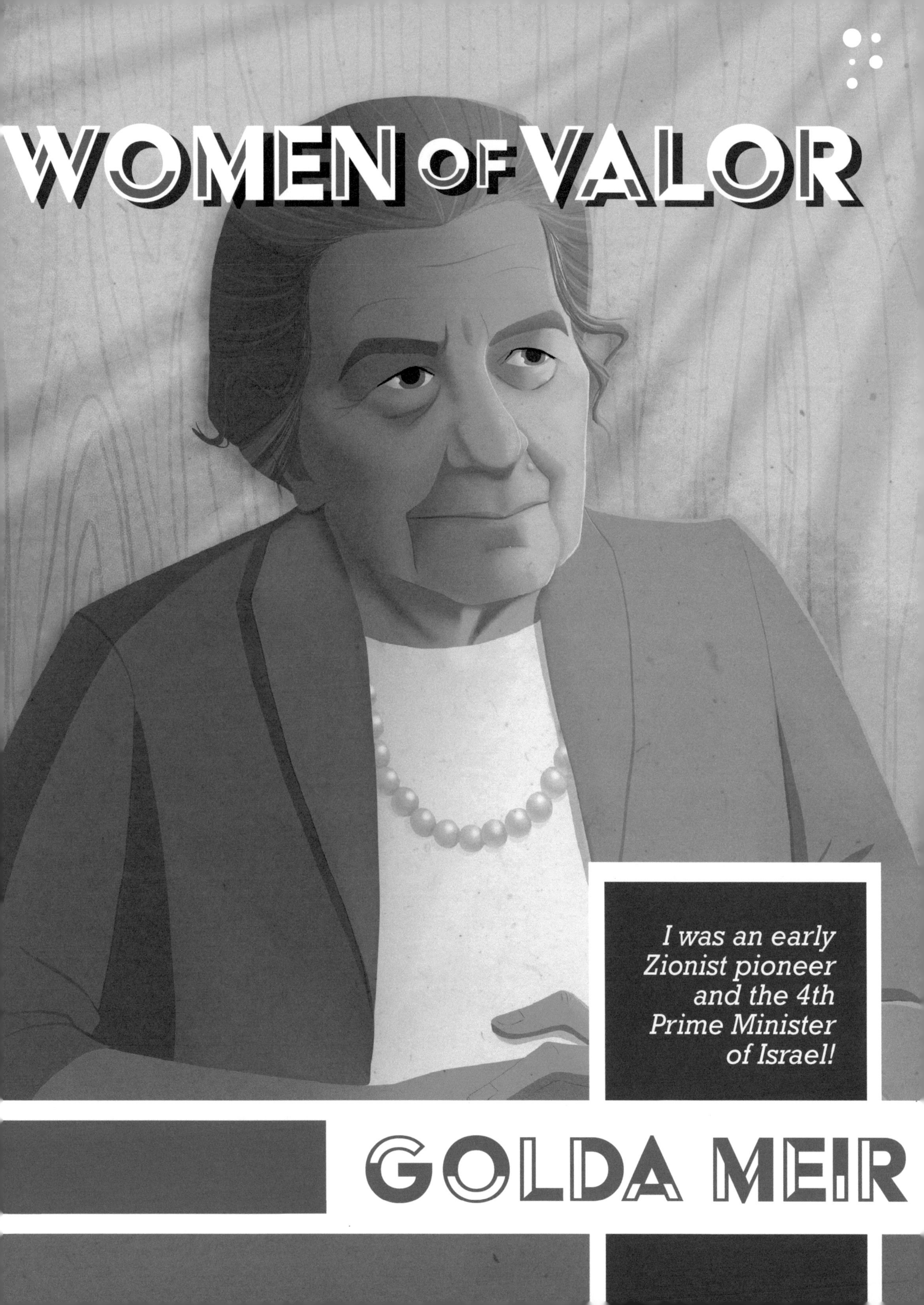
WOMEN OF VALOR
I was an early Zionist pioneer and the 4th Prime Minister of Israel!
GOLDA MEIR

Meet Golda Meir

One of Golda Meir's earliest memories helped shape the **trajectory** of her life. As a young girl, she watched her father nail boards across the windows of their tiny home in Kiev when neighbors warned of a coming **pogrom**. Although her family was spared, Golda always remembered the gripping fear she felt waiting for the attack.

Inspired by her older sister Shayna's activism, Golda concluded that personal responsibility and action were required to make her beliefs a reality. As a young woman, she embraced the Zionist movement and devoted her life to the struggle for a Jewish nation, often at great personal sacrifice.

Golda's strong convictions initially led her to Palestine to help settle the land. Later, she became a leader in the struggle for an independent Jewish state, serving in key government positions and ultimately as Israel's fourth prime minister.

At-a-Glance

- Born Goldie Mabovitch on May 3, 1898 in Russian Empire (present-day Ukraine

- A strong spokespersor for the **Zionist** cause.

- An early Zionist pioneer who helped develop and found the State of Israel.

- One of the signatories of Israel's Declaration of Independence in 1948.

- Israel's fourth prime minister (1969–74) and the first woman to hold the post.

- Known for her unwavering commitment to her convictions, no matter the personal sacrifice.

- Died December 8, 1978 in Jerusalem, Israel.

GETTY IMAGES

Young Golda

Golda was born one of Moshe and Bluma Mabovitch's eight children during a period of great unrest in Russia. The family was poor, hungry, and cold, and lived in constant fear of the Cossacks, the government's horse-mounted soldiers who terrorized villages in an effort to suppress **insurgents**.

Although Moshe's services as a master carpenter were in demand, he was rarely paid for his work because he was Jewish. Conditions became so harsh in Kiev that Moshe decided to emigrate to America. Unfortunately, he could only scrape together enough money for one ticket, so he went alone, promising to bring the entire Mabovitch family to America as soon as possible.

Meanwhile, Golda, her mother, and sisters relocated to the Jewish **ghetto** of Pinsk where they lived with her grandfather and worked in his tavern. At last, Golda had enough to eat, a comfortable place to live, and was surrounded by family. Yet, they still lived under constant fear of the Cossacks. In protest, Golda's older sister Shayna joined a secret Zionist movement and barely escaped arrest when her group was discovered by local authorities. Out of concern for Shayna's safety, Bluma insisted they immediately join Moshe in America.

Land of Opportunity

Golda and her family arrived in America in 1906, reuniting with her father in Milwaukee, Wisconsin. Golda was mesmerized by the crowded streets, cars, and stores with an abundance of food and brightly colored clothing. She especially loved school, where she quickly made friends and excelled in her studies. She remembered learning the "Pledge of Allegiance" in just a few days, enunciating each word carefully, so as not to race through it as her classmates did. The final words—*with liberty and justice for all*—meant the most to her, especially after her experiences in Russia.

Over time, Golda's family became deeply involved in their community. They attended discussion groups, clubs, and political meetings. They hosted intellectuals, political figures, and recent immigrants at their weekly Sabbath meals. Golda was also expected to help out by working in the small grocery store her mother opened in the front room of their house.

No matter how many hours Golda worked in the store, she continued to excel at school and was named valedictorian of her eighth grade class. Golda dreamed of attending high school and becoming a teacher, creating tension with her mother, who didn't believe that girls should be educated. Bluma wished for Golda to marry young and was determined to find her a suitable husband. When Golda refused to marry, Bluma insisted that Golda quit school. Out of desperation, Golda ran away from home and joined her older sister Shayna in Denver so she could continue her studies.

Seeds of Independence

Although Golda missed her parents, she was determined to follow her dreams. During her two years in Denver, Golda attended high school and became immersed in politics and philosophy. Shayna's friends talked of building a Jewish homeland in Palestine, sparking Golda's imagination. Her social life blossomed, but Golda was more interested in political causes than romance until she met a young man named Morris Meyerson.

Shayna felt responsible for her younger sister and began to worry when Golda spent less time studying and more time staying out late. The sisters began to argue frequently, so much so that Golda decided to move out. To afford living on her own, Golda gave up school and worked full-time in a department store. Still, she found time to be involved in political causes and followed reports of Jewish settlers moving to Palestine.

Moshe and Bluma were worried about Golda, so they invited her to return home and continue her studies.

> "It isn't really important to decide when you are very young just exactly what you want to become when you grow up … It is much more important to decide on the way you want to live."
>
> Golda Meir

The Zionist Dream

Back in Milwaukee, Golda returned to high school. She also became involved with the Zionist political group Poale Zion, and volunteered to teach Jewish heritage at the group's school. She continued to correspond with Morris, though he disapproved of her desire to immigrate to Palestine. When World War I broke out in Europe, Golda's family helped Jewish soldiers by raising money for food and clothing for the war's victims.

News reached Wisconsin that pogroms were taking place in Poland and Ukraine, causing Golda to grow more politically active. She organized local rallies and gave persuasive pro-Zionist speeches. More than ever, Golda believed that the Jewish people needed their own homeland, and she was determined to make that dream a reality by moving to Palestine. Morris believed that Golda's dream was merely a fantasy until 1917, when the British announced the Balfour Declaration, signaling official support for a Jewish state.

Kibbutz Life

Morris finally agreed to accompany Golda to Palestine, and they were married in 1917. Over the next few years, the couple worked diligently to raise money for their passage. In the Spring of 1921, they bid tearful farewells to their families, knowing that they might never see them again.

After an arduous journey, they arrived in Palestine, where they found a hot, dusty city and encountered American immigrants who were returning home because of the challenging life that Palestine offered. Yet, the horrible conditions did not deter Golda from her dream of settling the rugged land.

Golda applied three times for membership in **Kibbutz** Merhavia and was finally accepted in the Fall of 1921. All members were required to work—clearing and converting swampland into fertile farmland. Despite the grueling labor, Golda was delighted to live in this communal environment, but Morris struggled with the lack of privacy and possessions.

Golda continued to be very vocal about Zionist politics, and the kibbutz selected her to represent Merhavia at the kibbutz convention in 1922. Her impassioned speeches drew attention from Zionist party leaders, including the Pioneer Women, a worldwide Jewish women's welfare organization, who enlisted Golda to represent them in meetings with foreign dignitaries.

Major Changes

Due to Morris's health issues, he and Golda resettled in Jerusalem and welcomed two children. Golda later admitted her struggle with leading a traditional domestic life, claiming that the four years they lived in Jerusalem were the most miserable she had ever experienced.

By chance, Golda ran into an old friend who offered her a job with the Women's Labor Council. She gladly accepted the position even though it would require long hours, travel, and time away from home, marking a turning point in her life. She made the painful decision to separate from Morris and return to her longtime dream of actively building the Jewish state. She moved with her children to Tel Aviv, who also struggled with her long absences, highlighting the tension between the duty she felt for her country and her family obligations.

World War II

In 1933, Adolf Hitler rose to power and promised to rid Germany of the Jews, whom he blamed for all of Germany's problems. Within a few years, half of German Jews were fired from their jobs. Jewish homes and businesses were looted and reassigned to non-Jews. Many Jews were arrested and imprisoned. Because so many Jews wanted to leave Europe, world leaders convened to address the growing problem.

German citizens pass Jewish stores destroyed in Berlin during Kristallnacht, 1938.

By now, Golda had become a well-respected political leader in Palestine and was selected to attend the 1938 International Conference on Refugees in France. She was hopeful that other countries would help her people. She explained the terrible hardships that the Jews were suffering and begged other delegates to save them, but they offered only sympathy.

Soon, it was too late. When Hitler invaded Europe, the Jews were rounded up and forced into concentration and death camps. Over the course of World War II, six million Jews were killed in the Holocaust. After the war, the world reacted with shock as they learned of the horrors perpetrated by Hitler and his Nazi party.

17

Birth of a Nation

Golda called for the war refugees to be sent to Palestine immediately but was met with resistance from the British government, who did not want to anger the neighboring Arab nations. To her surprise, the British began to back away from the Balfour Declaration that had promised a path to Jewish statehood. The British government tightened its control over the area, but the Jews resisted and fought back.

As more shiploads of Jewish refugees came to Palestine, the British increased their forces, but it was not enough. In 1947, they deferred the whole problem of Palestine to the United Nations. Within months, the United Nations decided that Palestine would be divided into two independant nations—one Arab and the other Jewish.

The Jews erupted in joy, but the five neighboring Arab nations began to prepare for war in an effort to drive the Jews from the land. With an army of only 40,000 soldiers, Jewish leaders lacked the necessary resources.

Golda rushed to the United States, delivering powerful pro-Zionist speeches all across America to raise funds for the cause. In nearly three months, Golda raised $50 million to help equip the Jewish army.

On May 14, 1948, Golda's lifelong dream became a reality when the Jewish state in Palestine was officially established as Israel. Golda fought back tears as she signed her name to the Declaration of Independence.

GETTY IMAGES

A Natural Leader

Just one day later, five Arab armies attacked Israel. World leaders believed the war would end quickly because Israel was outnumbered, but the Jews persisted. They drove out the armies of Syria, Lebanon, and Egypt. The war ended when the United Nations helped negotiate a truce between Israel and the Arab nations.

Prime Minister Ben-Gurion asked Golda to serve as first Israeli ambassador to the Soviet Union and later, as Israel's Minister of Labor and Social Security. Golda became responsible for the welfare of every new immigrant to Israel. Seven years later, she was named Foreign Minister. By then, Golda had become one of the most well-known and beloved figures in all of Israel.

She retired from public office in 1966 and resumed a modest life as a private citizen, but everything changed when she learned of Prime Minister Levi Eshkol's sudden heart attack and death. The Israeli government needed a prime minister and once again called upon Golda.

Prime Minister Meir

Golda's five-year term as prime minister proved challenging. She faced the ongoing threat of war, in addition to domestic problems, including high **inflation**, labor shortages, and a wave of new immigrants. During her term, Israeli soldiers suffered grave casualties in the Yom Kippur War when they were attacked by Syria in the north and Egypt in the south.

GETTY IMAGES

Protesters demanded an investigation, citing the country's unpreparedness for the war. For the rest of her life, Meir regretted not acting earlier to protect more Israeli soldiers. She was later **exonerated** but ultimately held herself responsible for the loss of life. She officially left office in 1974 following a disengagement treaty with Syria.

In 1978, Golda succumbed to a 15-year battle with cancer. She had requested a simple funeral with no eulogies, yet nearly 100,000 people came to pay their respects. Throughout her life, Golda dreamed of peace for Israel and its neighbors, believing it was attainable as long as Israel remained strong.

Fascinating Facts about Golda

- When she married Morris, Goldie Mabovitch became Golda Meyerson. When Ben-Gurion encouraged her to adopt a Hebrew last name, she chose Meir, which in Hebrew means "illuminate."

- Golda formed *The American Young Sisters Society* to collect money to buy textbooks for schoolchildren who couldn't afford them.

- Golda's parents didn't think it proper for her to protest on street corners, but after witnessing one of her powerful speeches, her parents relented.

- Golda traveled over 300 miles disguised as an Arab woman to meet with King Abdullah of Trans-Jordan in an effort to dissuade him from joining other Arab states in a war against Israel.

- Golda was known for hosting late-night meetings in her kitchen. Israelis often commented that important government decisions were "cooked in Golda's kitchen."

Choosing What's Right

1. Golda Meir was deeply influenced by:
   - a. Fear of the pogroms and the Cossacks
   - b. Her older sister Shayna, who taught her to stand up for what was right
   - c. Zionist leaders who wanted to build a Jewish state in Palestine
   - d. All of the above

2. Golda and her family emigrated to America:
   - a. In 1903, settling in Madison, Wisconsin
   - b. In 1916, settling in Denver, Colorado
   - c. In 1906, settling in Milwaukee, Wisconsin

3. Eleven-year-old Golda and her friends formed *The American Young Sisters Society* to:
   - a. Collect money for a local theater troupe
   - b. Raise money for textbooks, for children who couldn't afford them
   - c. Raise funds for a local orphanage

4. Golda committed to following her dream of:
   - a. Becoming a teacher
   - b. Settling and building a Jewish homeland in Palestine
   - c. Marrying young and raising a family

5. As a member of Kibbutz Merhavia, Golda:
   - a. Cleared and drained the swampland for farming
   - b. Raised and cared for farm animals
   - c. Dug ditches, built roads, and planted trees

6. Golda served as a political leader in several key positions, including:
   - a. Minister of Finance, Foreign Minister, Prime Minister
   - b. Ambassador to the Soviet Union, Minister of Labor and Social Security, Prime Minister
   - c. Minister of Labor and Social Security, Minister of Defense, Prime Minister

Answer key in two pages

Crossword Puzzle

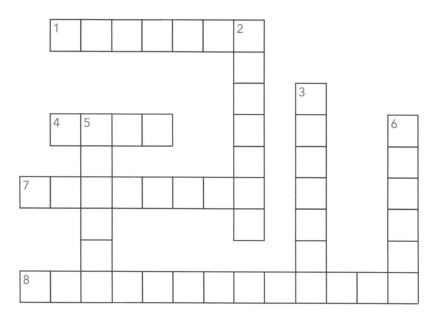

Answer key on next page

ACROSS

1. A collective community in Israel
4. The city where Golda was born
7. Violent mobs that swept through Russian towns to destroy property and attack Jews
8. Golda held this distinction in eighth grade

DOWN

2. Political movement that supports the state of Israel as the Jewish homeland
3. The British declaration that signaled a path to Jewish statehood
5. The name of the Jewish homeland, established in 1948
6. Golda determined that _____ was required to make her dreams a reality

Detect the Difference

Find the five differences in these nearly identical images of an Israeli banknote featuring Golda Meir. The back of the bill (shown on page 10) depicts a crowd of Russian Jews welcoming Golda as the first Israeli ambassador to the Soviet Union, with the verse "Let my people go" (Exodus 9:1).

Answer key on next page

Glossary

- **Trajectory**: A chosen path or course.

- **Pogrom**: (Russian for "devastation") A violent, government-condoned mob that swept through a town, destroying property and attacking Jews in Russia in the late 19th and early 20th centuries.

- **Zionist**: One who supports the preservation of Israel as the Jewish state, originally arising in the late 1800s with the goal of reestablishing a Jewish homeland in the region of Palestine.

- **Insurgent**: Rebelling against the leadership of a political party.

- **Ghetto**: A section of a city in which all Jews were required to live, due to discrimination.

- **Kibbutz**: An Israeli settlement rooted in the values of social responsibility, communal and cooperative living, and Jewish culture and tradition.

- **Inflation**: A steady increase in the level of consumer prices or a steady decline in the purchasing power of money.

- **Exonerate**: To free from blame.

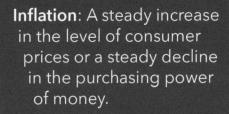

Sources

Davidson, Margaret. *The Golda Meir Story*. New York: Charles Scribner's Sons, 1976.

"Golda Meir." *Encyclopedia Britannica*, 29 Apr. 2021, https://www.britannica.com/biography/Golda-Meir.

Hitzeroth, Deborah. *The Importance of Golda Meir*. San Diego: Lucent Books, Inc., 1998.

Meir, Golda. *My Life*. New York: G. P. Putnam's Sons, 1975.

The American Heritage Dictionary of the English Language (online edition). Boston: Houghton Mifflin Harcourt.

CHOOSING WHAT'S RIGHT KEY: 1–d. 2-c. 3-b. 4-b. 5-a. 6-b.
CROSSWORD KEY: ACROSS: 1. KIBBUTZ. 4. KIEV. 7. POGROMS. 8. VALEDICTORIAN. DOWN: 2. ZIONISM. 3. BALFOUR. 5. ISRAEL. 6. ACTION

WOMEN OF VALOR

I was a best-selling author, and created my own philosophy!

AYN RAND

Meet Ayn Rand

Ayn Rand is a beloved author whose childhood experiences shaped the themes of her novels and ultimately led to the creation of her own **philosophy**.

Rand witnessed the **Bolshevik Revolution** and the Communist takeover of Russia. Ayn's family suffered years of severe poverty after armed soldiers confiscated her father's pharmacy. She escaped to the United States when she was 21.

Ayn pursued a writing career in Hollywood. She worked as a clerk and wrote stories, plays, and screenplays in her spare time. Her first novel, *We the Living*, introduced the idea that **individualism** is the source of freedom and **collectivism** is the root of oppression.

Rand is best known for her books *The Fountainhead* and *Atlas Shrugged*, which drew harsh critical reviews but became best-sellers. Although she was frustrated that her philosophy was not widely accepted, Rand influenced political movements including libertarianism and the Tea Party.

At-a-Glance

★ Born Alissa Rosenbaum February 2, 1905 in St. Petersburg, Russia.

★ Adopted the name Ayn Rand when she emigrated to the United States (Ayn rhymes with "pine").

★ Best known as the author of two novels, The Fountainhead (1943) and Atlas Shrugged (1957).

★ Developed her own philosophy, Objectivism: Every individual has a right to pursue the values that make him or her happy. It is morally wrong to sacrifice the self or others.

★ Influential among conservatives and libertarians from the mid-20th century.

★ Died March 6, 1982 in New York, New York.

Young Ayn (Alissa)

The eldest of three daughters, Alissa (the name Ayn was born with) was born in St. Petersburg, one of the most cultured cities in the world. Her family lived in a large apartment above her father's pharmacy. Her father had grown up poor and worked hard to support his family and put himself through university. He placed a high value on individualism.

Alissa taught herself to read and write before entering school. She enjoyed expressing her strong opinions and decided at age nine that she wanted to be a writer. In early 1917, when the revolution began with political demonstrations against the Russian monarchy, Alissa watched with fascination. She viewed politics as a **moral** issue. She felt that people should be free to set their own goals and not be forced to live by others' goals. In the beginning, Alissa was in favor of the revolution because it appeared to represent the fight for individual freedom. Russia had undergone a period of instability following World War I, and the government leaders were struggling to cope with political unrest, food shortages, and low morale. Government **corruption** was rampant, and Russians hoped for a better life.

However, life changed for the worse in October 1917 when the Bolsheviks seized power in Russia by occupying government buildings and other strategic locations. The prime minister fled, and soldiers filled the streets. Amid this unrest and fear, the Soviet regime was born. Private property, businesses, and banks were confiscated by the new government.

"To achieve, you need thought. ... You have to know what you are doing and that's real power."

Ayn Rand

Life Under Communism

Alissa remembered vividly when armed soldiers burst into her father's pharmacy and stamped a red seal on the door, indicating that it was now state-owned. In a single moment, Alissa's family lost nearly everything and was forced to live on their meager savings. She later wrote, "It was a horrible spectacle of brutality and injustice."

Alissa and her family moved to Crimea, where she attended high school and began writing her own short stories. She discovered author Victor Hugo, whose work had a profound influence on her own development as a writer. She admired that Hugo wrote about important issues through complex plots featuring heroic, larger-than-life characters. Alissa also enjoyed studying math because it was based on pure logic. She concluded that her values were "objective" because they were based on logic and reason.

Alissa studied history at the University of Petrograd. Soon after graduation, Alissa's family received a letter from a relative in the United States who had fled Russia in 1889 and knew about the horrors of the communist government. Alissa begged her mother to request their help in bringing her to America. In 1925, the Soviet government granted permission, and Alissa began her long journey, carrying only a small suitcase and her typewriter.

A PHILOSOPHY TO LIVE BY

Ayn Rand named her philosophy Objectivism. She believed that the only way to obtain knowledge was through rational thought, not faith or feelings, and that the creators of values are the greatest heroes of the human race.

Rand believed that something is good if it promotes human life (such as freedom, education, nutritious food), and evil if it destroys human life (such as political dictatorship, ignorance, poison).

She argued that the good must be based on objective fact, and not on the will of God, societal beliefs, or individual impulses.

Rand concluded that every human being should pursue values that advance his or her own happiness. Individuals succeed by following their values, not by surrendering them.

Life in America

Oscar White / Getty

Ayn (the name Alissa took after she arrived in America) first stayed with her mother's family in Chicago. They greeted Ayn warmly and asked about her life in Russia, but she refused to speak of it. Ayn wanted to focus on the future and was grateful for the opportunity of a new beginning. She later acknowledged that her mother's family had saved her life.

Ayn learned English by watching films in the small theater owned by her Aunt Sarah. She began writing screenplays in English and enlisted a young cousin to help her with English grammar.

In the summer, Ayn left for Hollywood to pursue a screenwriting career. Through her Aunt Sarah's connections, she was introduced to director Cecil B. DeMille's movie studio. By chance, DeMille noticed Ayn standing near the gate and offered her a ride to the studio where he was filming a new movie, *King of Kings*. He hired her to work as an extra on set. One week later, Ayn met her future husband, actor Frank O'Connor, whom she later married in 1929. They remained married until he died in 1979 and did not have any children.

"What you feel tells you nothing about the facts; it merely tells you something about your estimate of the facts."

Ayn Rand

Life as a Writer

Ayn wanted desperately to earn a living as a writer but struggled for several years, working as a junior screenwriter for Cecil DeMille and in the wardrobe department of RKO Pictures. In her spare time, Ayn developed her own screenplays and short stories. She also began writing her first novel, *We the Living*, about a young woman struggling to pursue her goals under communist rule in the Soviet Union.

Ayn sold a screenplay, *Red Pawn*, to Universal Studios for $700, allowing her to quit her job and focus entirely on the novel, which was published in 1936. *We the Living* was rejected by many publishers because the book was considered too intellectual and too political. No publisher wanted to earn a profit on a story that denounced the Soviet Union, but Ayn didn't give up and *We the Living* was finally published. Unfortunately, it was not initially well-received, but Ayn was determined to keep writing.

Ayn and her husband moved to New York when her courtroom drama, *Night of January 16th*, played for more than six months on Broadway. Around this time, Ayn also wrote a short story entitled *Anthem*, which tells the story of a young mind living in a **totalitarian** state where freedom of expression has been suppressed and the very idea of individualism stamped out.

Ayn also began working on her most famous literary works, *The Fountainhead* and *Atlas Shrugged*. In both books, Ayn explores the theme of individualism versus collectivism. Her heroes are independent thinkers whose lives are guided by their own minds, self-interests, and abilities.

Later Life

Atlas Shrugged was Rand's last work of fiction. It sparked controversy and launched the Objectivist movement, which has slowly entered mainstream American culture. In Ayn's later years, she concentrated on further developing Objectivism. She wrote many essays, gave lectures at universities, and appeared on television. In 1961, she published her first non-fiction book, *For the New Intellectual*. A lifelong smoker, Ayn suffered from lung cancer but ultimately died from heart failure in 1982. Her last book, *Philosophy: Who Needs It*, was published in 1982 just after her death.

Famous Books

Atlas Shrugged (1957)

- Synopsis: A future American society is on the brink of collapse under oppressive laws. A genius named John Galt decides to teach the world a lesson by convincing all the brilliant business leaders to go on strike. The world collapses without them. Under Galt's leadership, the leaders return to recreate the world according to Rand's philosophy of Objectivism.

- Rand defends the system of **capitalism** on moral grounds. She believes that pursuing one's own happiness is essential to living a moral life. Therefore, acting in one's own self-interest is morally correct, in contrast to making decisions based on self-sacrifice for the greater good. According to Rand, the only political system that supports individual freedom is capitalism.

- Published in 1957.

- Attacked by critics but became an instant best-seller.

The Fountainhead (1943)

- Synopsis: Howard Roark is an architect who designs a public housing project that is altered against his wishes by government officials. When he is tried in court, he stands for individualism, and the jury acquits him.

- Rand spent more than seven years working on the book.

- Initially rejected by 12 publishers; published in 1943.

- Now considered an American classic.

- Continues to sell more than 100,000 copies per year.

Fascinating Facts about Ayn

- When Ayn first arrived in the U.S., she lived with family in Chicago, where one of her relatives owned a movie theater. She visited the theater almost daily, watching films to hone her English skills.

- The name "Ayn" was inspired by the name of a Finnish writer. Ayn described her new surname as an abbreviation of Rosenbaum.

- Ayn became a U.S. citizen in 1931.

- When Ayn finally experienced financial stability in the 1930s, she tried to bring her family to the United States.

Unfortunately, the Soviet authorities did not grant the Rosenbaums permission to leave Russia. When World War II began, Ayn lost contact with her family.

- In the publishing industry, a novel usually shows its highest sales in the first few months following publication. Ayn's books reversed the pattern; sales were slow initially and gradually increased.

- Ayn stated that she wrote every page of the 1,000-page *Atlas Shrugged* a minimum of five times.

Free to Choose

1. Ayn Rand is best known as a:
   - ○ a. revolutionist
   - ○ b. writer
   - ○ c. actress

2. The Bolshevik Revolution ushered in:
   - ○ a. a period of peace and prosperity
   - ○ b. a democratic movement
   - ○ c. the rise of communism

3. The author who had a profound influence on Ayn was:
   - ○ a. Victor Hugo
   - ○ b. William Shakespeare
   - ○ c. George Sand

4. Ayn Rand named her personal philosophy:
   - ○ a. Individualism
   - ○ b. Collectivism
   - ○ c. Objectivism

5. Ayn's two best-selling novels are:
   - ○ a. *We the Living* & *The Fountainhead*
   - ○ b. *The Fountainhead* & *Atlas Shrugged*
   - ○ c. *Night of January 16th* & *Atlas Shrugged*

6. According to Ayn's philosophy of Objectivism, the individual should:
   - ○ a. sacrifice his own values for the sake of the greater good
   - ○ b. make decisions solely based on feelings
   - ○ c. pursue his own interests and values

Answer key in two pages

Crossword Puzzle

Answer key on next page

ACROSS

5. The name of the main character in *The Fountainhead*
7. The country where Ayn was born
8. What Ayn Rand called her philosophy

DOWN

1. Ayn left for America with a suitcase and this
2. The title of Ayn's first novel
3. Ayn believed that individuals should live according to these
4. The type of business owned by Ayn's father
6. Ayn learned English by watching these

Detect the Difference

Use your skills of observation to find the six differences in these nearly identical images of the Ayn Rand commemorative postage stamp, issued in April 1999. The stamp was designed by Phil Jordan of Falls Church, Virginia, and illustrated by Nicholas Gaetano of Fletcher, North Carolina.

Answer key on next page

©Olga Popova/123RF.COM

Glossary

- **Philosophy:** The study of the nature, causes, or principles of reality, knowledge, or values, based on logical reasoning.

- **Bolshevik Revolution:** The 1917 overthrow of the Russian government led by the Social Democratic Workers' Party (the Bolsheviks and Vladimir Lenin).

- **Individualism:** Belief in the primary importance of the individual and in the virtues of self-reliance and personal independence.

- **Collectivism:** The system of ownership and control of the means of production and distribution by a group, usually under the supervision of a government.

- **Moral:** Concerned with the judgment of right or wrong human action and character.

- **Corruption:** Dishonest or illegal behavior especially by powerful people

- **Totalitarian:** A form of government in which the political authority exercises absolute and centralized control over al aspects of life, the individual is secondary to the state, and all opposing expression is suppressed.

- **Capitalism:** An economic system in which the means of production and distribution are privately or corporately owned and growth occurs through the accumulation and reinvestment of profits gained in a free market. (PragerU: The individual pursues success to the best of his or her abilities)

Sources

Bernstein, Andrew. *Ayn Rand for Beginners*. Danbury: A For Beginners® Documentary Comic Book, 2009.

Biography.com Editors. "Ayn Rand Biography." *Biography.com*, 2 Apr. 2014, https://www.biography.com/writer/ayn-rand.

Branden, Barbara. *The Passion of Ayn Rand*. Garden City: Doubleday & Company, 1986.

Britannica, The Editors of Encyclopaedia. "Russian Revolution." *Encyclopedia Britannica*, 30 Oct. 2020, https://www.britannica.com/event/Russian-Revolution. April 2021.

Burns, Jennifer. *Goddess of the Market. Ayn Rand and the American Right*. New York: Oxford University Press, 2009.

Duignan, Brian. "Ayn Rand." *Encyclopedia Britannica*, 2 Mar. 2021, https://www.britannica.com/biography/Ayn-Rand.

Merriam-Webster Dictionary (online edition). April 2021.

Smithsonian National Postal Museum (https://postalmuseum.si.edu/people/ayn-rand). April 2021.

The American Heritage Dictionary of the English Language (online edition). Boston: Houghton Mifflin Harcourt.

FREE TO CHOOSE KEY: 1—b. 2-c. 3-a. 4-c. 5-b. 6-c.
CROSSWORD KEY: Across: 5. Howard Roark. 7. Russia. 8. Objectivism. Down: 1. typewriter. 2. We the Living. 3. values. 4. pharmacy. 6. movies.

WOMEN OF VALOR

I was the first woman to serve as Prime Minister of the United Kingdom!

MARGARET THATCHER

Meet Margaret Thatcher

Through hard work and determination, Margaret Thatcher rose from humble beginnings to become the first woman to lead a major Western democracy and one of the world's most influential politicians. She was the only British Prime Minister in the 20th century to serve three consecutive terms.

As leader of the **Conservative Party**, Margaret Thatcher reshaped the British economy and foreign policy at a time when many people believed Great Britain was in decline. She reduced the power of trade unions, privatized numerous government-run industries, lowered taxes, and cut welfare programs that encouraged joblessness. Her unique style and uncompromising political convictions came to be known as "Thatcherism."

During the **Cold War**, she defended democracy and took a hard line against **communism** and the Soviet Union. Margaret became one of the closest friends of Ronald Reagan, the 40th President of the United States.

Interesting Fact

- Born on October 13, 1925 in Grantham, Lincolnshire.

- First woman to serve as Prime Minister of the United Kingdom (1979-1990).

- Supported conservative views: limited government, free markets, nationalism, and individualism.

- Nickname: "The Iron Lady" (for her strong opposition to communism).

- Awarded the U.S. **Presidential Medal of Freedom** by President George H. W. Bush on March 7, 1991.

- Died April 8, 2013 in London.

GETTY IMAGES

Young Margaret

Margaret was born to Alfred and Beatrice Roberts in a small town in Eastern England. Her father was a Methodist preacher and owned a small grocery store.

Margaret and her older sister Muriel spent a lot of time helping out in the store. They worked behind the counter, slicing cheese and meat, weighing butter, and selling candies and cakes.

As Margaret's father became involved in local politics, the store became a meeting place for neighborhood people who shared his ideas. Margaret learned a lot about politics by listening to their conversations. She helped during local elections by addressing campaign pamphlets and attending local political meetings. Alfred Roberts served as a council member and eventually as Mayor of Grantham.

Margaret admired her father and was deeply influenced by his traditional values. He emphasized the importance of individual responsibility and self-reliance and taught her that life must be used for a noble purpose.

ALL IMAGES THIS PAGE: GETTY IMAGES

Margaret Thatcher on Leadership:

"Never follow the crowd. You work things out for yourself."

Education, Family, & Early Career

Margaret was a very serious student and attended Oxford University. She became involved in politics at the Oxford University Conservative
Association, where she honed her debating skills, met influential politicians, and served as one of the association's first women presidents.

After graduating with a degree in chemistry in 1947, Margaret worked as a research chemist at a plastics company. In her spare time, she volunteered at the local Conservative Party organization and was noticed by party leaders who recommended that she run for office in the nearby town of Dartford.

Margaret followed their advice and ran for Dartford's parliamentary seat in two separate elections in the early 1950s. Although she didn't win, she received a lot of publicity as the youngest woman candidate in the country. Running for office proved to be a good learning experience.

Around this time, Margaret met a wealthy businessman, Denis Thatcher. He shared Margaret's views and supported her political ambitions. They married in December 1951. Two years later, Margaret gave birth to twins Carol and Mark. She returned to school for legal training, specializing in taxation.

Margaret Thatcher on Women in Politics:

"In politics, if you want anything said, ask a man. If you want anything done, ask a woman."

Parliament

Margaret enjoyed her legal career and family life but had high ambitions to serve in public office. Her experience as a mother, tax lawyer, and housewife enabled her to relate to many different people. She searched for a district that would adopt her as a candidate, and was interviewed many times by Conservative Party officials but wasn't chosen.

Finally, in 1959, Margaret's persistence paid off. The London suburb of Finchley selected her to be their candidate, and she won the election, becoming one of the only women Members of **Parliament** (MPs) at the time. Over the next several years, Margaret was appointed to many leadership positions in the government, including Education Minister. She grew to become a powerful force in the Conservative Party.

After the Conservatives lost the majority in 1974, Margaret decided to run for leadership of the Conservative Party. In 1975, she was elected leader, making her the first woman to become Leader of the **Opposition**.

Around that time, Great Britain was experiencing great economic and political instability under the socialist-leaning Labour Government. The government was nearly bankrupt, unemployment was on the rise, and basic services, like power and garbage collection, were frequently interrupted.

When the Conservatives won the 1979 election, Mrs. Thatcher became Prime Minister of the United Kingdom. A new political star was born.

GETTY IMAGES

What is a Prime Minister?

A Prime Minister is the leader of a country with a parliamentary political system, like the United Kingdom. Each political party selects a leader from within its ranks. In a general election, the leader of the winning party is appointed Prime Minister by the Monarch (the King or Queen in some countries, including Great Britain), or a president (in countries like France and Israel). In contrast, American presidents are elected directly by the people (via the electoral college).

Prime Minister

Mrs. Thatcher delivered a clear message as she assumed office: she wanted to put the "Great" back into "Great Britain." The country was in decline and needed to return to order, efficiency, and individual responsibility. Thatcher believed that British citizens were beginning to believe more in government and less in themselves. Thatcher criticized **socialism** for depriving British people of their traditional liberties. While socialism offered privileges only to the top government leaders, capitalism extended greater opportunity to many more people.

Thatcher focused her efforts on economic recovery, but initially, her policies resulted in higher unemployment and lower wages. Despite the pain these changes brought at first, she stayed focused on her long-term goal. She did not want Great Britain to become a socialist country, and she strove to empower individual citizens.

Thatcher cut welfare programs that encouraged joblessness and allowed government-owned utilities to be privately owned. Over time, as the economy improved, peoples' lives improved, and she became more popular.

In 1982, Prime Minister Thatcher faced a major foreign crisis when Argentina invaded the British Falkland Islands off the coast of South America. She tried to resolve the crisis using diplomacy, but when it didn't work, she directed British troops to go to war to defend the Falklands. It was a risky move because Britain was still in the middle of its economic recovery, and war is expensive. But in just 10 days, Great Britain won the war and returned the islands to British control. Thatcher's decision to defend the Falklands was very popular with the British people and helped her win re-election in 1983.

REUTERS

Margaret Thatcher on Socialism:

"There is no such thing as public money. There is only taxpayers' money."

Domestically, Thatcher sought to limit the power of the trade unions because she believed they didn't allow their members to have a say in important decisions. In 1984, she stood her ground in a year-long miners' strike. Her government protected workers who wanted to go to work, even when the miners' union insisted on closing the mines. Her government applied pressure to the unions by fining them when they held illegal strikes. A year later, when the union had been defeated, the miners gradually returned to work.

In foreign policy, Thatcher became an important leader in the Cold War. She and U.S. President Ronald Reagan took a unified and tough stance against communism. Thatcher strongly supported President Reagan's Cold War policies. She improved Britain's relations with **reformist** Soviet leader Mikhail Gorbachev, which helped end the Cold War peacefully, without ever firing a shot.

During her third term as Prime Minister, Thatcher sought to reform England's socialized medical system and create a standard educational curriculum. She also tried to implement a fixed rate local tax, which was very unpopular, even in her own party. Widespread public protests erupted against her tax policy.

Her Conservative Party colleagues feared that her tax policies were going to prevent them from winning the next elections. In 1990, under pressure, Thatcher resigned her position as Prime Minister.

Retirement

Thatcher served as a Member of Parliament until she retired in 1992. After retirement, she became a public speaker and wrote several books about her experience in politics. She suffered a number of small strokes before her death in 2013.

Fascinating Facts about Margaret

- Young Margaret's family lived in an apartment above her father's grocery store in Grantham. The apartment didn't have running water or an indoor toilet!

- In 1939, Margaret's family helped a young Jewish girl named Edith escape Austria after Hitler took over. Edith lived with the Roberts family and shared what life was like living as a Jew under an anti-Semetic regime. Young Margaret was shocked.

- Before becoming Prime Minister, Thatcher underwent speech training to lower her pitch and perfect a calm tone.

- Thatcher became known as "Thatcher, the milk snatcher" for ending a government-sponsored free milk program during her tenure as Education Minister

- Thatcher survived an assassination attempt on October 12, 1984, when a bomb exploded at the hotel where she was staying.

REUTERS

Fill-in-the-Blank

1. In 1925, Margaret Roberts was born in the town of _____, the second of two children.

2. Margaret attended _____, where she earned a degree in chemistry.

3. Margaret later became a tax lawyer, but she really aspired to be a _____.

4. Margaret's conservative political views were initially inspired by her _____.

5. Mrs. Thatcher created a sensation when she became the first _____ Prime Minister in British history.

6. As Prime Minister, Margaret Thatcher embraced policies that gave _____ more freedom.

7. Mrs. Thatcher earned the nickname "_____" because she took a very strong position against communism.

Answer key in two pages

WordScramble

MRIEP EINRTSMI ☐☐☐☐☐ ☐☐☐☐☐☐☐☐

NROVTCVEAIES ☐☐☐☐☐☐☐☐☐☐☐

AITSRTEHCMH ☐☐☐☐☐☐☐☐☐☐

DGNANEL ☐☐☐☐☐☐☐

LCDO WRA ☐☐☐☐ ☐☐☐

RNMPIELATA ☐☐☐☐☐☐☐☐☐

DFXORO YVIREUSTIN ☐☐☐☐☐☐ ☐☐☐☐☐☐☐☐☐☐

ICEEOTNL ☐☐☐☐☐☐☐☐

AGATMERR ☐☐☐☐☐☐☐☐

ITOISCPL ☐☐☐☐☐☐☐☐

Answer key on next page

Write Your Campaign Slogan!

A political campaign slogan is a brief statement that describes what your campaign is about. Margaret Thatcher's 1950 campaign slogan was "Vote Right to Keep What's Left."

Imagine that you are running for public office. What cause is important to you? What causes are important to your friends and your community?

Glossary

- **Conservative Party:** A political party that promotes traditional views, especially in the United Kingdom or Canada.

- **Cold War:** A state of political tension between nations that stops short of full-scale war, especially that which existed between the United States and Soviet Union following World War II.

- **Communism:** A system of government in which the state plans and controls the economy and a single authoritarian party holds power, claiming to make progress toward a higher social order in which all goods are equally shared by the people.

- **Presidential Medal of Freedom:** An award given by the U.S. president to recognize people who have made an especially significalnt contribution to the security or national interests of the United States or world peace.

- **Parliment:** The national legislature of the United Kingdom, made up of the House of Lords and the House of Commons. When people in Great Britain vote, the elect Members of Parliment (MPs) and those MPs vote for the Prime Minister.

- **Opposition:** The act of resisting. The Opposition party is the party not currently in power.

- **Socialism:** A system or condition of society in which the means of production are owned and controlled by the state/government.

- **Reformist:** A person who promotes change of an existing system.

Sources

Biography.com Editors. "Margaret Thatcher Biography." *Biography.Com*, 2 Apr. 2014, www.biography.com/political-figure/margaret-thatcher

Ducksters. "Biography for Kids: Margaret Thatcher." *Ducksters*. Technological Solutions, Inc. (TSI), www.ducksters.com/biography/world_leaders/margaret_thatcher.php. March 2021.

"Margaret Thatcher Foundation." *Margaret Thatcher Foundation,* www.margaretthatcher.org. March 2021.

Meir, Maayan. "Margaret Thatcher and the Jews." www.aish.com/jw/s/Margaret-Thatcher-and-the-Jews.html.

Moskin, Marietta D. *Margaret Thatcher of Great Britain.* New Jersey: Julian Messner, 1990.

The American Heritage Dictionary of the English Language (online edition). Boston: Houghton Mifflin Harcourt.

Young, Hugo. "Margaret Thatcher." *Encyclopedia Britannica*, 9 Oct. 2020, https://www.britannica.com/biography/Margaret-Thatcher. March 2021.

FILL-IN-THE-BLANK ANSWER KEY: 1. GRANTHAM. 2. OXFORD UNIVERSITY. 3. POLITICIAN. 4. FATHER. 5. WOMAN. 6. INDIVIDUALS. 7. IRON LADY

WORD SCRAMBLE KEY: 1. PRIME MINISTER. 2. CONSERVATIVE. 3. THATCHERISM. 4. ENGLAND. 5.COLD WAR. 6. PARLIAMENT. 7. OXFORD UNIVERSITY. 8. ELECTION. 9. MARGARET. 10. POLITICS.

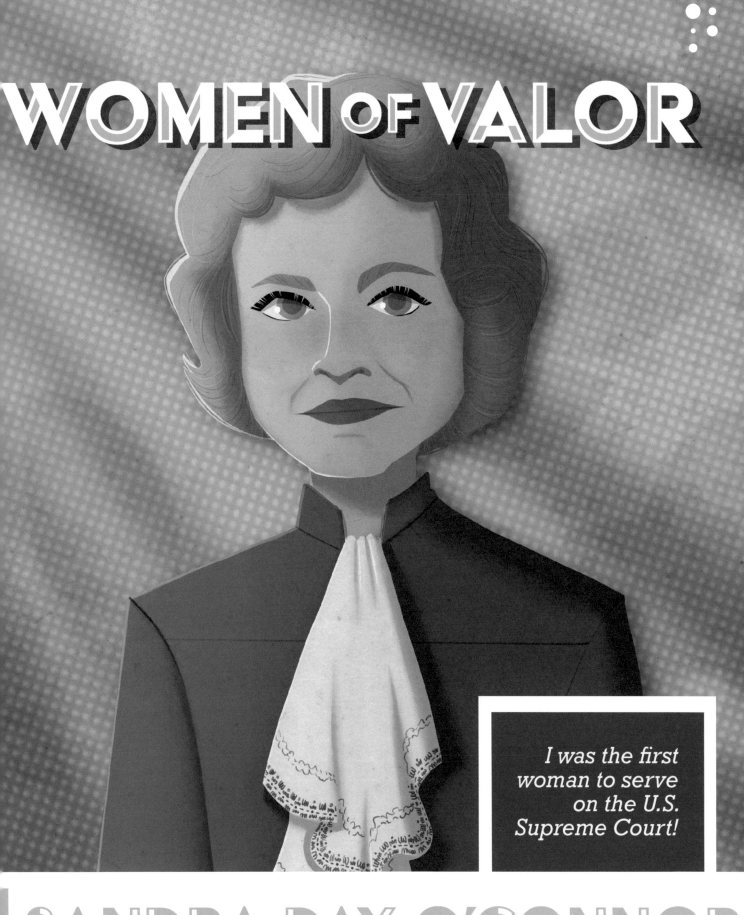

WOMEN OF VALOR

I was the first woman to serve on the U.S. Supreme Court!

SANDRA DAY O'CONNOR

Meet Sandra Day O'Connor

Many have called Sandra Day O'Connor the "most important woman in American history." An Arizona cowgirl, mother, lawyer, and judge, she broke new ground when she was sworn in as the first woman on the U.S. Supreme Court in 1981.

Because the legal profession had traditionally been a male domain, Sandra's **ascension** to the nation's highest court shattered gender barriers, and she became an instant celebrity and inspiration to women across the country.

However, Sandra's rulings often surprised the women activists who assumed she would always side with them. Affirming her commitment to fairness, Sandra insisted, "My power on the Court depends on the strength of my arguments, not on my gender."

During her nearly 25 years on the Court, Sandra was regarded as an independent thinker and a leader. She played a pivotal role in many decisions and left a lasting impact on the United States.

At-a-Glance

★ Born Sandra Day on March 26, 1930 in El Paso, Texas.

★ Served as Arizona state senator and as a judge on the Maricopa County Superior Court and Arizona Court of Appeals.

★ First woman to serve on the U.S. Supreme Court, as associate justice from 1981 to 2006.

★ Known for her intelligence and grit, **meticulously** researched opinions, and moderate conservative views.

★ Author of five books, including two children's books, based on her childhood experiences.

★ Awarded the Presidential Medal of Freedom by President Barack Obama in 2009.

Humble Beginnings

The oldest of Harry and Ada Mae Day's three children, Sandra grew up on her family's cattle ranch, the Lazy B. The ranch straddled Arizona and New Mexico and was 35 miles from the nearest town, so Sandra had an **atypical** upbringing. She passed her days with the farm animals and the cowboys who worked on the ranch. From an early age, she participated in ranch chores and learned how to ride a horse, repair a fence, drive a truck, and shoot a rifle. Sandra also spent a lot of time reading books from her parents' library.

Because Sandra was eight years older than her next sibling, Ann, she received the attention of an only child. She remembers fondly her father's genuine interest in her and appreciated their strong bond over the years. She recalls spending hours at the dinner table with him, discussing ranching, politics, and economics. Sandra looked up to her mother as a strong female role model who made the hard ranch life look easy. She taught Sandra how to read and play many card games.

To ensure that Sandra received the best possible education, her parents made the difficult decision to send her to a private school in El Paso, Texas. So, at age five, she went to live with her grandmother, Mamie Wilkey, returning to the ranch only during the summers.

"I don't know that there are any shortcuts to doing a good job."

Sandra Day O'Connor

GETTY IMAGES

Ranch Life

The Lazy B was isolated, rugged, and expansive at roughly 250 square miles, and Sandra's family had few luxuries. The ranch had no electricity or running water until she was seven. Meals consisted mostly of beef, beans, dried fruit, and biscuits. The Southwestern climate was unforgivingly hot and dry, and flies were a constant nuisance. Sandra recalls how her family would watch the skies, always hoping for rain.

Although there weren't other children around, Sandra and her siblings had the unique opportunity to grow up alongside their parents and learn valuable life lessons, particularly about the significance of hard work and **self-reliance**.

They often rode horseback for hours in the heat and dust and drove around in their father's truck, performing tedious tasks such as examining the cattle, checking the grass, oiling the windmills, and repairing the water wells.

Sandra also learned from the cowboys who spent their entire lives on the ranch and babysat her as a child. From Rastus, she learned to do the best she could with what she had. From Jim, she learned to focus on results, not excuses. From Bug, she learned to see the humor in every situation, and from Claude, she learned to set high standards and be precise in every job she set out to do.

Despite the challenging ranch conditions, Sandra always missed the Lazy B when she was away. Living on a cattle ranch was an unusual experience, one that she greatly appreciated throughout her life.

Education & Marriage

In El Paso, Sandra excelled at the Radford School for Girls, where she graduated at age 12. She continued to be a stand-out student at Austin High School, while also participating in the student yearbook and various school clubs. Her loving grandmother impressed upon her that she could accomplish anything she set out to do.

At age 16, Sandra entered Stanford University in California to study economics and discovered her true calling when she took a class taught by law professor Dr. Harry J. Rathbun in her third year. Sandra was so inspired that she applied for early admission to Stanford Law School. She graduated third in her law class, two places behind her friend William H. Rehnquist, who also went on to become a Supreme Court justice.

Sandra met fellow student John Jay O'Connor when they were assigned to edit a *Stanford Law Review* article together. They got along so well that they went out every night for six weeks. Eager to introduce John to her family, Sandra invited him to the Lazy B. Although John was more of a city boy, he endeared himself to everyone at the ranch with his great sense of humor. Soon after the visit, the couple announced their engagement and were married at the Lazy B in December of 1952.

Early Career & Family

GETTY IMAGES

When Sandra graduated from Stanford Law School in 1952, she was surprised to discover that law firms would not hire women lawyers. Her only job offer was to work as a legal secretary, a position that did not match her qualifications. She later gained experience as a civilian attorney in Germany when John was stationed there as a lawyer for the United States Army.

Sandra later recalled that "in 1957, many women were not being hired in major law firms," so she opened up her neighborhood law office in Arizona. She also hoped for job flexibility while caring for her newborn son,

Scott. To help pay the law firm's rent, Sandra and her partner handled every case that came through the door, which provided her exposure to many different kinds of cases.

Sandra and John soon welcomed two more sons, Brian and Jay. To balance motherhood and work, Sandra initially worked part-time but eventually took a few years off to take care of the boys while they were young. With her two older boys in school, Sandra returned to work as a lawyer in the Arizona attorney general's office, gradually extending her hours to full-time. During this time, she became more involved in politics and began volunteering for conservative political causes.

Accomplished Lawyer, Politician, and Judge

In 1969, the Arizona Republican Party asked Sandra to fill a vacant seat in the Arizona Senate, making her one of only two women to serve in that role. She held the position until 1975, twice earning reelection. She was also selected by her colleagues to be the senate's majority leader, the first woman in the U.S. to earn that title.

Although she enjoyed political life, Sandra returned to the legal profession when she was elected as a trial court judge for the Maricopa County Superior Court. As judge, she listened to trials about crimes, contracts, and other legal matters. She quickly earned a reputation for being both fair and demanding.

Arizona Governor Bruce Babbitt promoted Sandra to serve as a judge on the Arizona Court of Appeals. She found the work challenging and rewarding and imagined it would be her job for life, but another opportunity soon presented itself.

Sandra Day O'Connor is sworn in as Supreme Court Justice by Chief Justice Warren Burger. Her husband, John O'Connor, looks on.

Supreme Court Justice

In July 1981, Sandra received a call from the White House and an invitation to meet with President Ronald Reagan. He was considering candidates to fill Potter Stewart's seat on the U.S. Supreme Court. To her surprise, President Reagan called Sandra a few days after their meeting to offer her the nomination. She later learned that he had been so impressed with her that he had not interviewed any other candidate for the position.

Upon receiving a president's Supreme Court nomination, the U.S. Senate must hold public hearings to interview a candidate regarding his or her qualifications, political views, and legal experience. Sandra did her best to answer the senators' questions during three intense days of questioning. When the senators voted, she was confirmed unanimously. On September 25, 1981, Sandra was sworn in by Chief Justice Warren Burger as the first female associate justice and the 102nd member of the United States Supreme Court.

Notable Cases

During Sandra's **tenure** on the Court, the justices were mostly aligned along partisan lines and could be counted on to vote with their like-minded colleagues. Sandra often found herself in the middle, enabling her to cast the swing vote. She helped shape U.S. history in several landmark cases, including:

Bush v. Gore (2000): Sandra cast the deciding vote in the historic 5-4 decision to uphold the Florida secretary of state's original certification of Florida's electoral votes—effectively naming George W. Bush the 43rd president.

Grutter v. Bollinger (2003): In another 5-4 decision, the Court upheld an **affirmative action** program at the University of Michigan. "In order to cultivate a set of leaders with legitimacy in the eyes of the citizenry," Sandra said, "it is necessary that the path to leadership be visibly open to talented and qualified individuals of every race and ethnicity."

Hamdi v. Rumsfeld (2004): In a 6-3 decision, the Supreme Court declared that even citizens designated "enemy combatants" have the right to challenge their imprisonment. Sandra wrote the Court's opinion, asserting that "a state of war is not a blank check… when it comes to the rights of the nation's citizens."

Retirement and Beyond

Sandra retired on January 31, 2006 and was succeeded by Justice Samuel Alito. As a measure of her influence, when Sandra attended Stanford Law School in the 1950s, only two percent of law students were women at the time. By the time she retired in 2006, that percentage had risen to 48 percent.

Following retirement, Sandra returned to Arizona to devote more time to her family. She later established the Sandra Day O'Connor Institute for American Democracy to advance civic learning and engagement.

In 2018, she announced that she had been diagnosed with the beginning states of dementia and would be retiring from public life.

Fascinating Facts About Sandra

- Early in her career, Sandra volunteered to work for free at the San Mateo County Attorney's office. She was hired for a paid position as soon as one became available.

- Sandra was a self-described "compulsive volunteer," performing public service for many groups, including the Salvation Army, the Arizona State Hospital, and local schools.

- Sandra became a founder of both the Arizona Women Lawyers Association and the National Association of Women Judges.

- Sandra was inducted into the Cowgirl Hall of Fame in Fort Worth, Texas in 2002.

- In 2005, Sandra wrote *Chico*, a book about her beloved childhood pet horse and other adventures on the Lazy B.

- In 2009, Sandra founded the Sandra Day O'Connor Institute for American Democracy to advance civil discourse, civic engagement, and civics education.

You Be the Judge

In her work as a Supreme Court justice, Sandra Day O'Connor was required by the Constitution to fairly and impartially apply the law—not the law as she wanted it to be, but as it was written. Now that you've read about Sandra Day O'Connor, how would you decide on the following questions? Vote Yay or Nay.

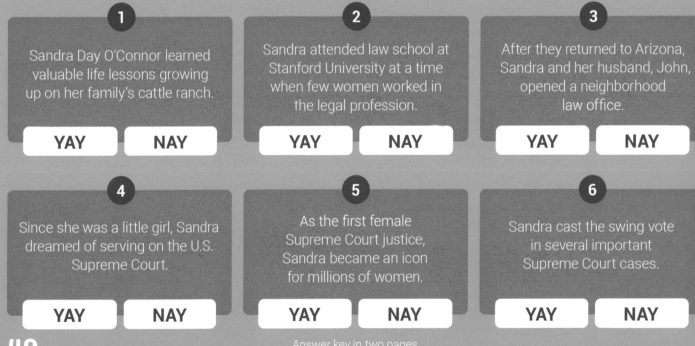

1

Sandra Day O'Connor learned valuable life lessons growing up on her family's cattle ranch.

YAY · NAY

2

Sandra attended law school at Stanford University at a time when few women worked in the legal profession.

YAY · NAY

3

After they returned to Arizona, Sandra and her husband, John, opened a neighborhood law office.

YAY · NAY

4

Since she was a little girl, Sandra dreamed of serving on the U.S. Supreme Court.

YAY · NAY

5

As the first female Supreme Court justice, Sandra became an icon for millions of women.

YAY · NAY

6

Sandra cast the swing vote in several important Supreme Court cases.

YAY · NAY

Answer key in two pages

Word Search

ARIZONA
COWGIRL
RANCH
STANFORD
SENATOR
REAGAN
JUSTICE
CHICO
CIVICS
WOMAN
HISTORY
REPUBLICAN

Answer key on next page

```
R H I S T O R Y T W B R
S E Y N X N C I V I C S
T V P R L T A C N E T W
A X L U R R O G C L D X
N V M P B W M I A A T X
F S X N G L T O N E G J
O Q E I A S I O C R R Y
R L R N U M Z C R I D Q
D L Z J A I O A A R H W
V G Y R R T N W D N J C
K M V A P C O R Y D J D
D G L J H R W R R T M G
```

"The Roundup" Writing Exercise

Growing up on her family's cattle ranch, Sandra worked alongside quiet, busy adults who expected her to be independent and help with the chores. She later noted that her unusual background helped prepare her for a career in law.

1. How do you think that Sandra's early experiences enabled her to succeed in the legal profession? In life?

2. What is the connection, if any, between ranching and working as a Supreme Court justice?

3. Does any part of your life resemble Sandra's childhood experiences? How is it the same? How is it different?

Glossary

- **Ascension:** To move upward; rise.

- **Meticulous:** Acting with extreme care for details.

- **Atypical:** Not usual or normal.

- **Self-Reliance:** Dependence on one's own efforts, judgment, and abilities.

- **Tenure:** The period or term of holding something in one's possession, such as an office or occupation.

- **Affirmative Action:** A government strategy that favors certain minority groups—who have faced past discrimination—for employment and educational opportunities.

- **Dementia:** A condition marked by loss of memory, concentration, communication, and abstract thinking, resulting from brain injury or from a disease such as Alzheimer's disease.

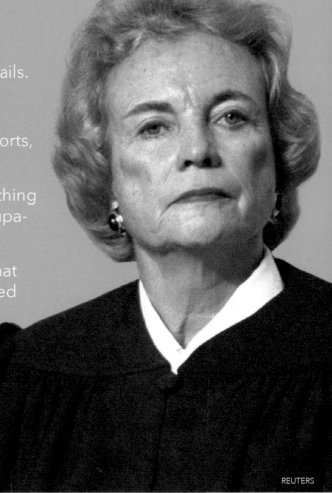

REUTERS

Sources

The American Heritage Dictionary of the English Language (online edition). Boston: Houghton Mifflin Harcourt.

Bales, Scott. "Justice Sandra Day O'Connor: No Insurmountable Hurdles." *Stanford Law Review*, Vol. 58, No. 6, 2006, pp. 1705–1711. www.jstor.org/stable/40040327. Accessed September 2021.

Biography.com Editors. "Sandra Day O'Connor Biography." https://www.biography.com/law-figure/sandra-day-oconnor. Accessed September 2021.

Bodine, Laurence. "Sandra Day O'Connor." *American Bar Association Journal*. Vol. 69, No. 10 (October, 1983), pp. 1394-1398. http://www.jstor.org/stable/20756478.

McFeatters, Ann Carey. *Sandra Day O'Connor: Justice in the Balance*. New Mexico: University of New Mexico Press, 2005.

O'Connor, Sandra Day. *The Majesty of the Law: Reflections of a Supreme Court Justice*. New York: Random House, 2003.

O'Connor, Sandra Day and H. Alan Day. *Lazy B: Growing Up on a Cattle Ranch in the American Southwest*. New York: Random House, 2002.

"Research Library and Archives by The Sandra Day O'CONNOR INSTITUTE." *Sandra Day O'Connor Institute*, http://oconnorinstitute.org/civic-programs/oconnor-history/sandra-day-oconnor-policy-archives-research-library/.

Smentkowski, Brian P. "Sandra Day O'Connor." *Encyclopedia Britannica*, 22 Mar. 2021, https://www.britannica.com/biography/Sandra-Day-OConnor. Accessed September 2021.

YOU BE THE JUDGE KEY: 1–Y. 2–Y. 3–N. 4–N. 5–Y. 6–Y.

 **PragerU**

For more kids content, visit **PragerUkids.com**

WOMEN OF VALOR

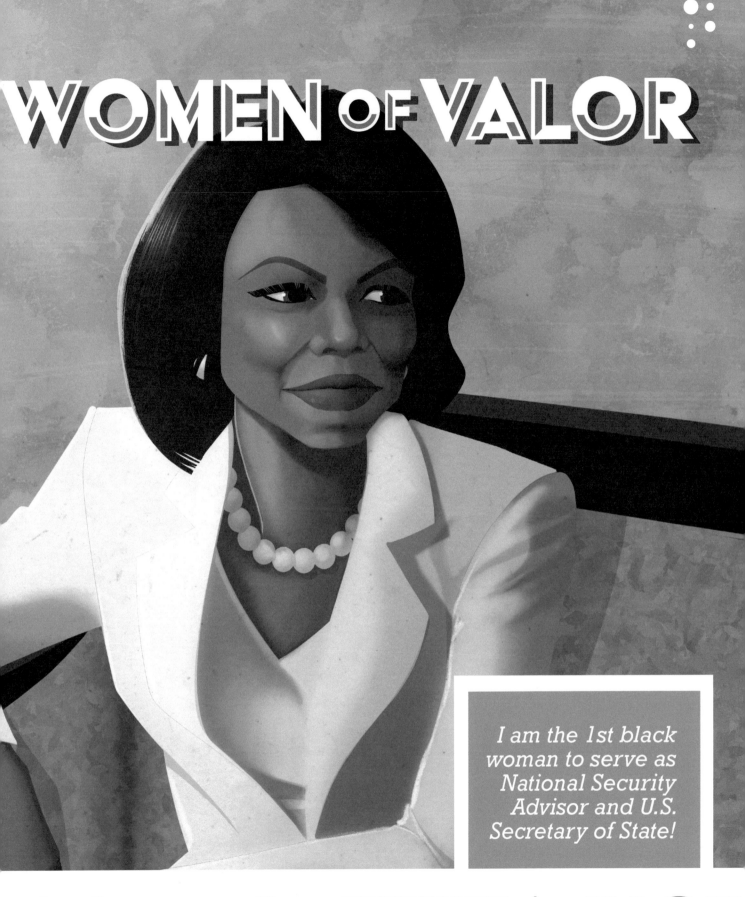

I am the 1st black woman to serve as National Security Advisor and U.S. Secretary of State!

CONDOLEEZZA RICE

Meet Condoleezza Rice

Condoleezza Rice grew up the only child of highly educated, devoted parents who strongly encouraged her to achieve success despite facing obstacles such as **segregation** and **racism**.

Since many people at the time were prejudiced against black Americans, Condoleezza (often shortened to "Condi") worked diligently to be twice as smart and twice as talented as her white peers. She excelled academically, skipping two grades and starting college part-time at age 15, while still in high school. Condi's first love was playing the piano, but she also found time to become a competitive figure skater, practice ballet, and study French.

Eventually, Condi's driven nature led her to earn a doctorate in international studies, rise to leadership at Stanford University, and accept high-ranking positions in the White House.

As Secretary of State, Condoleezza promoted freedom in her "Transformational Diplomacy" initiative. She believed that if the U.S. created diplomatic partnerships with other nations, they might adopt American values, form democratic governments, and secure greater freedom for their citizens.

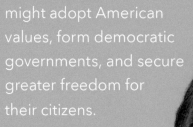

At-a-Glance

⭐ Born Condoleezza Rice on November 14, 1954 in Birmingham, Alabama.

⭐ Condoleezza's mother created her unique name by combining the Italian musical terms *con dolce* and *con dolcezza*, meaning "with sweetness."

⭐ Served as **provost** of Stanford University for six years.

⭐ First black woman to serve as both National Security Advisor (2001–05) and Secretary of State (2005–09) to U.S. President George W. Bush.

⭐ Known for being firm, decisive, and self-confident, even during tough negotiations.

Young Condoleezza

John and Angelena Rice, Condi's parents, shielded their daughter as much as possible from the racial turmoil around her and taught her that she could do and be whatever she wanted.

They were very involved in their community. John was a Presbyterian minister and guidance counselor, and Angelena taught high school students science, speech, and music. They believed that education, hard work, and properly spoken English would protect Condoleezza–even against the racism in Birmingham and across America.

Over the years, Condoleezza's parents made many financial sacrifices to afford piano, ballet and skating lessons, and private high school. They wanted to provide Condoleezza with the best opportunities for success. Indeed, her family on both sides highly valued education and the arts. Condoleezza's paternal grandfather had earned a scholarship to become a Presbyterian minister. He founded many churches and schools and visited poor neighborhoods nearby, urging parents to send their kids to college. Even though they never met, Condoleezza credits him as a "guiding presence" in her life, having given her the "gift of transformation through education."

The Rice family was incredibly close. They discussed political issues and made decisions together as a family. Condoleezza often engaged in **theological** debates with her father, who encouraged her to use reason and intellect to explore her faith.

Although Condoleezza grew up in the segregated South, she became convinced that racism was "their" problem, not hers. She always felt supported by her parents, extended family, teachers, and her church community. Looking back, she says that the message in her small community was clear: *We love you and will give you everything we can to help you succeed. But there are no excuses, and there is no place for victims.*

ear-old Condoleezza Rice's school picture, 1961

"Differences can be a strength rather than a handicap."

Condoleezza Rice

GETTYIMAGES

Instability in Birmingham

Racial tensions intensified in Condi's hometown as people began to protest against the racist **Jim Crow** laws that kept black and white Americans separate in public areas. Activists marched in demonstrations and boycotted businesses that supported segregation. Birmingham transformed into a dangerous place of hatred, prejudice, and violence against blacks.

White mobs called "night riders" terrorized black families in their communities, setting off bombs to intimidate blacks who were pushing back against Jim Crow laws. Violence reached a peak when the **Ku Klux Klan (KKK)** detonated a bomb at a neighborhood church, killing four young girls on their way to Sunday school, one of whom was Condoleezza's friend. The bombing captured the nation's attention and ultimately led to the **Civil Rights Act** of 1964, ending legal segregation.

A New Life Out West

Although life slowly improved in Birmingham with segregation's end, the Rice family moved west when Angelena's father was offered positions at Stillman College in Tuscaloosa and later at the University of Denver.

In Denver, Condi discovered a passion for figure skating. She skated competitively, placing third in one competition. She admits that she wasn't great, but that the sport taught her discipline and **perseverance**. Condoleezza also won statewide and regional piano competitions and played Mozart with the Denver Symphony. She continued to excel in school and entered the University of Denver part-time during her senior year of high school, when she was just 15.

Condoleezza seemed destined to become a concert pianist, but after exposure to more advanced musicians, she realized that while she was talented, she would never be a great **virtuoso**. So, she left the music program and sought a field where she would shine.

Condoleezza took a class in international politics with Josef Korbel, a former Czech diplomat who founded the Graduate School of International Studies. She credits him with "opening an entirely new world" to her. He encouraged her to follow her interest in international politics and become a Soviet specialist. She learned Russian and studied the Soviet military. At 19, Condi graduated *cum laude*. A year later, she earned her master's degree from the University of Notre Dame and returned to Denver to earn her doctorate in international studies in 1981. She helped pay her tuition by teaching piano.

Early Career

Dr. Condoleezza Rice joined the staff of Stanford University, where she became a popular lecturer on civil-military relations, Soviet policy in the third world, and elite politics. A few years later, she won the Walter J. Gores Award for Excellence in Teaching, became a fellow at the Hoover Institution, and wrote many articles and two books on Soviet and Eastern European foreign and defense policy. Dr. Rice credits much of her early success to getting to know key leaders at Stanford who served as mentors.

In 1985, she was awarded a fellowship at the prestigious Council on Foreign Relations and offered a yearlong position with the Joint Chiefs of Staff. She worked for the Nuclear and Chemical Division, analyzing situations in which the United States might use its nuclear forces. One of her highlights was doing a presentation in "the Tank," the place where all-important military decisions are made.

Condoleezza witnessed and helped shape many of the great historic events unfolding in the Soviet Union and Eastern Europe. Her in-depth studies had made her an expert on the Soviet Union. ABC News invited Dr. Rice to provide on-air commentary about U.S.-Soviet relations, launching her into the national spotlight.

When President George Herbert Walker Bush was elected in 1989, he invited Condoleezza to join the National Security Council. She accompanied President Bush to a meeting with Soviet leader Mikhail Gorbachev. He introduced her by saying, "This is Condoleezza Rice. She tells me everything I know about the Soviet Union."

The Cold War

After World War II, the United States and the Soviet Union engaged in a long political standoff known as the Cold War, a troubling period for Americans who feared nuclear war and the growing threat of communism. Because both nations possessed weapons of mass destruction (WMDs), they were capable of destroying one another. To address the threat, the U.S. offered aid and bolstered its influence in Western Europe, while the Soviets established communist regimes in Eastern Europe. Ultimately, they avoided direct military confrontation, engaging only in operations to prevent their allies from defecting.

During the 1980s, President Reagan successfully challenged Soviet leader Mikhail Gorbachev. Through Reagan's efforts, freedom was restored to communist East Germany when the Berlin Wall fell. By 1991, the Soviet Union had dissolved, and the Cold War had come to an end.

Road to the White House

Dr. Rice returned to Stanford to become the university's youngest provost at age 38. In her role, she was responsible for 1,400 professors, 14,000 students, and a budget of $1.5 billion. She also involved herself locally, founding the Center for a New Generation, an after-school enrichment program for kids in East Palo Alto, CA. Like her grandfather and father, Condoleezza wanted to help kids and families appreciate the value of education.

Dr. Rice was on track to become Stanford's next president but decided to step down so that she could help Texas Governor George W. Bush prepare for his presidential campaign. After Bush won, he appointed her as National Security Advisor. In her new role, Condoleezza counseled him on world events, attended Cabinet meetings, and met with foreign diplomats.

GETTY IMAGES

September 11th

On September 11, 2001, al-Qaeda terrorists hijacked four planes and attacked the World Trade Center in New York and the Pentagon in Washington, D.C. President Bush and Dr. Rice decided to respond with military action against the Taliban, the ruling party in Afghanistan who had harbored the terrorists. After defeating Afghanistan's government, the Bush administration shifted its focus to Iraq, believing that the regime helped terrorists and might have WMDs. Condoleezza became a staunch defender of the controversial war against Iraq as a means to stop Iraqi dictator Saddam Hussein from developing and using WMDs.

Secretary of State and Beyond

When President Bush was reelected, he named Dr. Rice to serve as the 66th Secretary of State. She advanced a doctrine of "Transformational Diplomacy," traveling widely to expand and strengthen U.S. diplomatic relations. In her confirmation hearing, she stated, "We must use American diplomacy to help create a balance of power in the world that favors freedom."

She advised the president on foreign affairs and worked with other nations on issues such as trade and nuclear weapons. She also worked tirelessly to negotiate peace between Israel and the Palestinians.

When Bush's second term ended, Condoleezza returned to Stanford University, and has since received several honorary degrees from various American universities. Today, she serves as director of the school's Hoover Institution, a public-policy **think tank**.

GETTY IMAGES

"There cannot be an absence of moral content in American foreign policy. Europeans giggle at this and say we are naive, but we are not European, we are American and we have different principles."

Condoleezza Rice

Fascinating Facts about Condoleezza

- Condoleezza's great-grandmother, Julia Head, was a freed slave who learned how to read.

- Condi's parents tried to enroll her in first grade when she was only three years old.

- Condoleezza remembers her father holding a shotgun as he stood watch nightly on her childhood front porch. He didn't believe that he could rely on the police to protect his family from night riders. To this day, Condi is a fierce defender of the **Second Amendment**.

- Condi and her family took a trip to Washington, D.C. when she was ten years old. Staring at the White House, she remarked, "One day, I'll be in that house."

- Condoleezza has played the piano at diplomatic events at embassies, including a performance for Queen Elizabeth II.

Fill-in-the-Blank

1. In 1954, Condoleezza Rice was born in _____, the only child of John and Angelena Rice.

2. Condoleezza excelled in school and entered college at _____ when she was only 16.

3. Condoleezza was an accomplished _____ and looked forward to a career in music.

4. One of Condi's early mentors was _____, a Czech diplomat who introduced her to the field of _____ _____.

5. Condoleezza had a strong feeling she'd be in the White House someday. She served in two high-ranking positions in President George W. Bush's administration: _____ and _____.

6. Condoleezza championed a diplomacy initiative referred to as _____.

Answer key in two pages

Word Scramble

NOACEELZDOZ

BNMRIMHGIA

VLCII GSIRHT

ANIPO

AECTIOUDN

VTISOE OUNNI

DLACPOYMI

EHITW EUSOH

NFOGERI CLPOIY

RPOOTVS

Answer key on next page

Noteworthy Considerations Writing Exercise

Throughout her busy career as a diplomat, Condoleezza continued to play the piano to help ground her in challenging times. Consider the following questions:

1. When have you worked really hard to achieve a goal?

2. What keeps you calm and focused when you're under pressure?

3. Condoleezza learned how to read music before she learned how to read books. American poet Henry Wadsworth Longfellow wrote, "Music is the universal language of mankind." Do you agree with his assertion? Why or why not?

GETTY IMAGES

Condoleezza Rice and cellist Yo-Yo Ma perform during the National Endowment for the Arts National Medal of Arts Awards ceremony, April 22, 2002 in Washington, D.C.

Glossary

- **Segregation**: The institutional separation of people of different races, classes, or ethnic groups, especially as a form of discrimination.

- **Racism**: The belief that race determines differences in human character or ability and that a particular race is superior to others.

- **Provost**: A university administrator of high rank.

- **Theological**: Relating to the study of God and religious truth, practice, and experience.

- **Jim Crow**: State and local laws in the U.S. South, in effect from the late 19th century until the 1960s, that discriminated against black people, treating them as second-class citizens.

- **Ku Klux Klan (KKK)**: A violent secret society organized in the South after the Civil War to uphold white power.

- **The Civil Rights Act of 1964**: A bill signed into law by President Lyndon B. Johnson that ended discrimination based on race, color, religion, or national origin.

- **Perseverance**: Consistent effort in a course of action despite difficulties, failure, or opposition.

- **Virtuoso**: A person with exceptional skill, technique, or talent in the arts, such as music.

- **Think Tank**: An institution organized to study and advocate for certain government policies in various fields, such as the military, economics, or education.

- **Second Amendment**: An amendment to the U.S. Constitution, adopted in 1791 as part of the Bill of Rights, guaranteeing citizens the right to keep and bear arms.

Sources

Biography.com Editors. "Condoleezza Rice." *Biography.Com*, 19 Jan. 2021, www.biography.com/political-figure/condoleezza-rice. Accessed June 2021.

"Cold War." *Encyclopedia Britannica*, 21 Jun. 2021, https://www.britannica.com/event/Cold-War. Accessed July 2021.

"Condoleezza Rice." *Encyclopedia Britannica*, 2 Mar. 2021, https://www.britannica.com/biography/Condoleezza-Rice. Accessed June 2021.

Cunningham, Kevin. *Journey to Freedom: Condoleezza Rice*. Mankato, MN: The Child's World, 2009.

Rice, Condoleezza. *A Memoir of My Extraordinary, Ordinary Family and Me*. New York: Delacorte Press, 2010.

Robinson, Peter. "Condoleezza Rice—Piano in My Life." *Piano Performer Magazine*. 21 June, 2016.

The American Heritage Dictionary of the English Language (online edition). Boston: Houghton Mifflin Harcourt. July 2021.

U.S. Department of State. http://www.state.gov/secretary/index.htm.

Wade, Linda R. *Condoleezza Rice*. Delaware: Mitchell Lane Publishers, Inc., 2003.

Page 3 photo: https://www.al.com/news/birmingham/2015/05/condoleezza_rice_has_traveled.html

FILL-IN-THE-BLANK ANSWER KEY: 1. BIRMINGHAM, ALABAMA. 2. UNIVERSITY OF DENVER. 3. PIANIST. 4. JOSEF KORBEL, INTERNATIONAL STUDIES. 5. NATIONAL SECURITY ADVISOR, SECRETARY OF STATE. 6. TRANSFORMATIONAL DIPLOMACY.

WORD SCRAMBLE KEY: 1. CONDOLEEZZA. 2. BIRMINGHAM. 3. CIVIL RIGHTS. 4. PIANO. 5. EDUCATION. 6. SOVIET UNION. 7. DIPLOMACY. 8. WHITE HOUSE. 9. FOREIGN POLICY. 10. PROVOST.

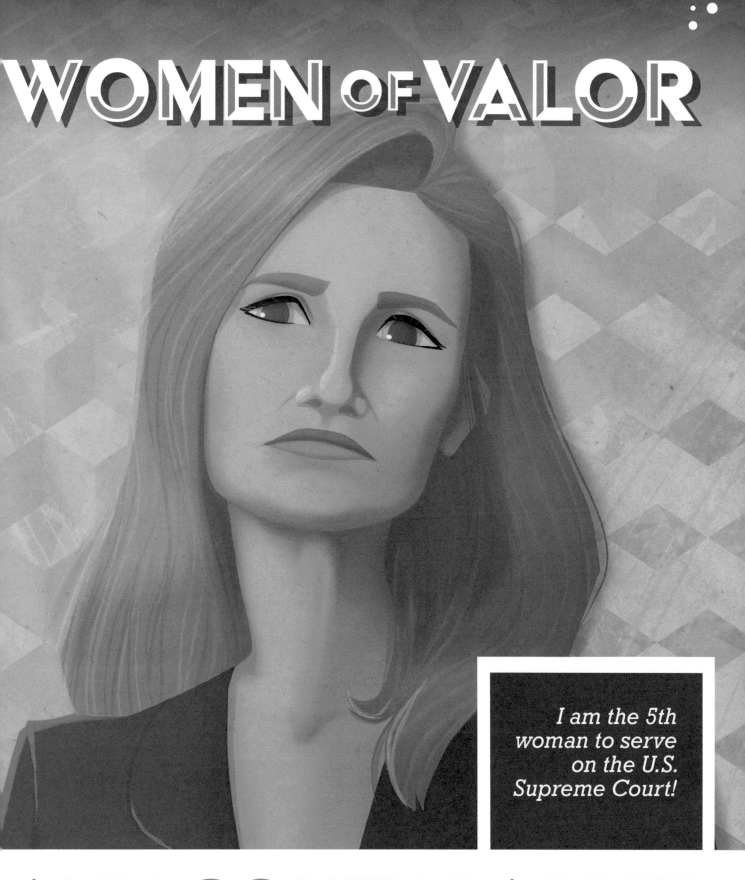

WOMEN OF VALOR

I am the 5th woman to serve on the U.S. Supreme Court!

AMY CONEY BARRETT

Meet Amy Coney Barrett

Amy Coney Barrett is the 115th Justice of the U.S. Supreme Court, succeeding Justice Ruth Bader Ginsburg. She is well prepared for her job, having honed her skills as a judge on the U.S. Court of Appeals for the Seventh Circuit and as a professor at Notre Dame Law School.

Amy also learned about the law by clerking for Supreme Court Justice Antonin Scalia. He was a major influence on Amy's life, and she later said, "His judicial philosophy is mine, too." Like Scalia, Justice Barrett is an **originalist**, believing that the Constitution should be interpreted according to its meaning at the time it was adopted. In her Supreme Court confirmation hearing, Barrett said: "A judge must apply the law as it is written, not as she wishes it were."

At-a-Glance

⭐ Born Amy Vivian Coney on January 28, 1972 in New Orleans, Louisiana.

⭐ 115th Justice and fifth woman to serve on the U.S. Supreme Court.

⭐ Mother of seven children, including two children adopted from Haiti and one with Down syndrome.

⭐ A role model for women, Amy excelled in school and in her career while embracing a religious life and raising a family.

Young Amy

Amy Coney was raised in a big family in rural Old Metairie, Louisiana. She is the eldest of seven children, with five sisters and one brother. Her mother, Linda, was a homemaker and taught French at a local high school, and her father, Michael, was a lawyer for Shell Oil Company.

The Coneys are a devout Roman Catholic family, instilling in Amy a strong faith and the values of hard work and integrity. Her father still serves as an ordained deacon at his church in Old Metairie, and her family has been involved in the Christian organization the People of Praise.

Amy attended Catholic schools and was a standout student. She impressed her classmates at St. Mary's Dominican High School so much that they elected her class vice president. She worked just as hard at Rhodes College in Tennessee and graduated with honors in English literature and French in 1994.

Amy wanted to serve others through a legal career, so she enrolled at Notre Dame Law School. Not surprisingly, she was very successful there, too, and was named the top student in her class, graduating *summa cum laude* (with the highest distinction).

"What greater thing can you do than raise children? That's where you have your greatest impact on the world."

Amy Coney Barrett

Early Career

After graduation, Amy jumped straight into law, serving as a clerk for Judge Laurence Silberman of the U.S. Court of Appeals in Washington, D.C. She then got her big break when she clerked at the highest court in the land, the U.S. Supreme Court, for her mentor Justice Scalia. As a clerk, Amy worked very hard every day to make sure the judges were prepared to make decisions about important cases.

Amy went on to work at a **prominent** law firm in Washington, D.C. Her professional success helped launch her career in academia as a law professor at George Washington University and Notre Dame. Amy soon emerged as a serious scholar of constitutional law and became such a valued instructor that she was recognized three times as Notre Dame's "Distinguished Professor of the Year."

As Amy's popularity at Notre Dame grew, more people wanted to hear what she had to say. She was known for her strong **conservative** and Catholic beliefs and became a respected voice for originalism. Many legal groups, like the Alliance Defending Freedom and the Federalist Society, regularly invited her to their events. At these events, she spoke to excited young law students and attorneys who shared her belief in limited government and individual liberty, ideas that are central to the U.S. Constitution.

A Large Family

In 1999, Amy married another lawyer from Notre Dame, Jesse M. Barrett. They went on to form their own large family of nine, believing that raising children would be their most significant impact on the world. Two of their seven children were adopted from Haiti, and their youngest child was born with special needs.

Like millions of Americans, Jesse and Amy work hard to raise and provide for their children while also having successful careers. Amy credits her success to teamwork with her husband and his aunt, who helped with in-home childcare for 16 years. She also remembers keeping a toy box in her office at Notre Dame so that her daughter Emma could be with her while she was at work. Amy has remarked that flexible workplaces—those that allow children to come to the office—can help working mothers.

USA TODAY NETWORK VIA REUTERS CONNECT

Circuit Court Judge

President Donald Trump recognized Amy's brilliance as a legal thinker. In May 2017, he nominated her to serve on the U.S. Court of Appeals for the Seventh Circuit, which hears cases from Illinois, Indiana, and Wisconsin. The U.S. Senate confirmed her for the Court on October 31, 2017. During her three years in the Seventh Circuit seat, Judge Barrett authored nearly 90 opinions.

In one case in 2019 (*Kanter v. Barr*), Amy's fellow judges on the Seventh Circuit decided that people who had previously gotten into trouble with the law couldn't own a gun, but she disagreed. She wrote a **dissenting** opinion, arguing that the plain meaning of the Second Amendment grants Americans—even those who have committed **felonies**—the right to own guns to protect themselves, especially if they haven't committed a violent crime.

In another 2019 case (*Doe v. Purdue University*), Amy and her fellow justices heard a case where Purdue University violated a student's right to **due process** and suspended him for a year. She and the rest of the court protected the student's rights by deciding the case in his favor.

"We shouldn't be putting people on the court that share our policy preferences. We should be putting people on the court who want to apply the Constitution."

Amy Coney Barrett

Supreme Court Justice

Amy's remarkable work on the Seventh Circuit led President Trump to nominate her to replace the late Justice Ruth Bader Ginsburg on the U.S. Supreme Court. The President praised Amy as a "woman of unparalleled achievement, towering intellect, sterling credentials and unyielding loyalty to the Constitution."

Although many Americans support originalism, some do not, and they did not want Amy to be appointed. They feared that if Amy were confirmed to the Supreme Court, it might become more conservative.

During Amy's confirmation hearings, Democrat senators tested her on many controversial issues like abortion rights, climate change, immigration, same-sex marriage, and the Affordable Care Act. Many of them were also concerned about the potential influence of her strong Catholic faith. Amy calmly listened and responded to their questions, insisting, "I am fully committed to equal justice under the law for all persons."

Impressed by her record and intelligence, the Senate **Judiciary** Committee voted unanimously to advance Amy's nomination to the Supreme Court. On October 26, 2020, the Senate confirmed Amy to the Supreme Court in a 52-48 vote, strengthening the Court's conservative majority. She was sworn in by Justice Clarence Thomas.

First Supreme Court Term

In *Roman Catholic Diocese of Brooklyn v. Cuomo (2020)*, her first case on America's highest court, Amy decided to uphold the religious rights of all Americans. She and a majority of her colleagues on the Court struck down Governor Andrew Cuomo's COVID-related restrictions that prevented people from worshiping God as they saw fit.

She wrote her first majority opinion in the 2021 case *U.S. Fish and Wildlife Service v. Sierra Club*, where she put limits on what documents people can access from the government.

As Amy has only been a Supreme Court justice for a short time, her full influence is not yet known. Her judicial philosophy will be further revealed in future cases on the Affordable Care Act, voting rights, gun rights, abortion, and religious liberties.

In Brief: The U.S. Supreme Court

When was the Supreme Court formed?
The Court took shape with the passage of the Judiciary Act of 1789 and initially had six justices.

How many justices serve on the Supreme Court?
The Court is made up of nine justices, including one Chief Justice and eight associate justices. According to the Constitution, Congress determines the number of justices. Since the Judiciary Act of 1869, there have been nine justices.

How does someone become a justice?
The President nominates someone for a vacancy on the Court and the Senate votes to confirm the nominee, which requires a simple majority.

Can anyone serve as a Supreme Court justice?
The Constitution does not specify qualifications such as age, education, profession, or native-born citizenship. A justice does not have to be a lawyer, but all have been trained in the law.

Do justices have term limits?
No. They can only be removed from office by impeachment.

How many cases does the Court hear each term?
The Court receives approximately 7,000-8,000 petitions each term but only hears oral arguments in about 80 cases.

Do all justices need to be present to hear a case?
A **quorum** of six justices is required to decide a case.

What words are written above the main entrance to the Supreme Court building?
"EQUAL JUSTICE UNDER LAW"—These words express the ultimate responsibility of the U.S. Supreme Court.

Fascinating Facts about Amy

- Amy was designated by faculty members as the most outstanding graduate in her undergraduate college's English department.

- Barrett is one of three sitting Supreme Court justices to have worked on landmark case *Bush v. Gore* in 2000, prior to their appointment on the Court. The case ultimately decided the 2000 presidential election, awarding Florida's 25 electoral college votes to Republican candidate George W. Bush.

- Barrett's daughter, Vivian, was adopted from Haiti at the age of 14 months and weighed just 11 pounds. The Barretts were told that she might never walk normally or talk, but she has overcome these challenges and is very athletic.

- Amy and her husband debated for years whether one parent should stay home to raise their children. She has described "soul-searching and anxiety about balancing kids and work."

- In October 2017, Barrett was out trick-or-treating with her children just an hour before she was voted into the Seventh District Court of Appeals by the U.S. Senate.

You Be the Judge

As a Supreme Court justice, Amy Coney Barrett conducts rigorous research and legal analysis in order to apply the law fairly in the court cases she hears. Now that you've read about Amy Coney Barrett, how would you decide on the following questions? Vote Yay or Nay.

1
Amy Coney Barrett was born and raised outside New Orleans, Louisiana.

YAY   NAY

2
Amy Coney Barrett worked as a law professor at Rhodes College in Tennessee.

YAY   NAY

3
Amy and her husband Jesse have seven children, including two children they adopted from Jamaica.

YAY   NAY

4
Amy was deeply influenced by Supreme Court Justice Antonin Scalia.

YAY   NAY

5
Amy is an originalist, meaning that she applies her own original ideas to every case she hears.

YAY   NAY

6
President Donald J. Trump nominated Amy for the U.S. Court of Appeals for the 7th Circuit, and three years later, for the Supreme Court.

YAY   NAY

Answer key in two pages

Word Search

ORIGINALIST
PROFESSOR
JUDGE
SUPREME COURT
CONSTITUTION
DISSENT
DUE PROCESS
MOTHER
LOUISIANA
CATHOLIC
CONSERVATIVE
SCALIA

```
C O N S E R V A T I V E L V V K
Y M O P L J Y C Q R P R M L D L
T Q I J M P D W A R M P Z O M L
A R T K P Z W U J T W N R X D N
N P U V B L K X E R H I P J J N
A V T O N R G M Z P G O W N T T
I Z I L C B O M D I R J L Y K R
S D T M X E G S N I S O U I Z T
I M S L O X M A S D S C C D C Q
U N N T R T L E K E N S A E G X
O Y O R V I H L R J F W E L S E
L K C M S T J E Y P T O G N I S
D Q P T L Q B P R Q U J R Y T A
W T R N N R J M M G N S D P B R
```

Order in the Court! Writing Exercise

1. The U.S. Constitution is the law of the land in the United States. Pick an amendment, summarize it, and explain why you think the Founding Fathers included it in our Constitution.

2. Write your own opinion on an important topic. Be sure to research both sides before coming to a conclusion.

Glossary

- **Originalist**: One who believes that the U.S. Constitution should be interpreted based on the authors' intent at the time it was adopted.

- **Prominent**: Widely and popularly known.

- **Conservative**: One favoring traditional views and values.

- **Dissenting**: Differing in opinion, especially from the majority.

- **Felony**: A serious crime like murder or robbery, punishable by a severe sentence, such as imprisonment for more than a year.

- **Due Process**: An established course for judicial proceedings designed to protect the legal rights of the individual.

- **Judiciary**: A system of courts of law for the administration of justice.

- **Quorum**: The minimum number of members of a group or organization who must be present to transact business legally.

Sources

"5 things you need to know about Amy Coney Barrett," *South Bend Tribune*, 27 Sept. 2020, https://www.southbendtribune.com/news/local/5-things-you-need-to-know-about-amy-coney-barrett/article_79a482ca-fbc0-11ea-8f70-b3134dc4bab7.html.

"About the Court: General Information." *Supreme Court of the United States*, www.supremecourt.gov/about/faq_general.aspx.

"Barrett, Amy Coney." *Biography.com*, 28 Sept. 2020, https://www.biography.com/law-figure/amy-coney-barrett.

Canaparo, GianCarlo, and John Malcolm. "The Triumph of Justice Amy Coney Barrett." *The Heritage Foundation*, 27 Oct. 2020, www.heritage.org/courts/commentary/the-triumph-justice-amy-coney-barrett.

Golding, Bruce. "Amy Coney Barrett: Mother of 7, Woman of Faith, Who Says Religion Has No Place in Rulings." *NY Post*, 26 Sept. 2020, nypost.com/2020/09/26/amy-coney-barrett-woman-of-faith-who-says-religion-has-no-place-in-rulings.

Houck, Aaron M. "Amy Coney Barrett." *Encyclopedia Britannica*, 24 Jan. 2021, https://www.britannica.com/biography/Amy-Coney-Barrett. Accessed May 2021.

"ICYMI: Grassley To Support Judge Barrett's Nomination To Supreme Court." Press Release from Office of Senator Church Grassley, 24 Oct. 2020, https://www.grassley.senate.gov/news/news-releases/icymi-grassley-support-judge-barrett-s-nomination-supreme-court.

Johnson, K.C. "Returning Due Process to Campus." *City Journal*, 17 Jul. 2019, https://www.city-journal.org/john-doe-v-purdue-univ.

Liptak, Adam. "Splitting 5 to 4, Supreme Court Backs Religious Challenge to Cuomo's Virus Shutdown Order." *New York Times*, 26 Nov. 2020, https://www.nytimes.com/2020/11/26/us/supreme-court-coronavirus-religion-new-york.html.

Richard, Michael S. *Biography of Amy Coney Barrett: An Interesting Life History of Amy Coney Barrett the 115th Associate Justice of the United States Supreme Court*. Kindle Edition, 2020.

Slattery, Elizabeth and Bates, Tiffany. "Amy Coney Barrett, in Her Own Words." *The Heritage Foundation*, 28 Sept. 2020, https://www.heritage.org/courts/commentary/amy-coney-barrett-her-own-words.

Stimson, Charles "Cully." "These 4 Immigration Opinions Demonstrate Amy Coney Barrett's Faithful Adherence to the Law." *The Heritage Foundation*, 6 Oct. 2020, www.heritage.org/courts/commentary/these-4-immigration-opinions-demonstrate-amy-coney-barretts-faithful-adherence.

The American Heritage Dictionary of the English Language (online edition). Boston: Houghton Mufflin Harcourt. May 2021.

Whelan, Ed. "Judge Barrett's Dissent in Second Amendment Case." *National Review*, 3 Mar. 2019, https://www.nationalreview.com/bench-memos/judge-barretts-dissent-in-second-amendment-case.

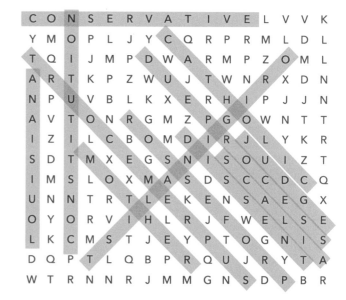

YOU BE THE JUDGE KEY: 1–Y. 2-N. 3-N. 4-Y. 5-N. 6-Y.

READY FOR MORE?

Experience all the **FREE CONTENT** PragerU Kids has to offer!

STREAM FREE SHOWS ON YOUR TV OR TABLET

Download our FREE mobile or TV app to stream every PragerU Kids show! Or, watch any time at PragerUkids.com.

ENJOY HOURS OF FREE SHOWS

Browse over 300 educational videos for K-12, including game shows, cartoons, and inspiring reality shows.

EXPLORE WHOLESOME STORIES & AMAZING HISTORY

Download free e-books at PragerUkids.com or purchase printed copies on Amazon.

FREE RESOURCES FOR TEACHERS & PARENTS

Supplement your child's viewing experience with lesson plans & worksheets that meet educational standards.

Made in United States
Troutdale, OR
09/15/2024

22834553R00045